Body
IN
Space

Body
IN
Space
*My Life
with Tammy*

MARGARET GONZALEZ

Body in Space

Names followed by an asterisk have been changed by the author to protect the identity of those involved.

ISBN: 978-0-578-43520-6

Cover Design and Page Layout by Hannah Nichols Creative, www.hannah-nichols.com

For Don

ACKNOWLEDGMENTS

I am very grateful to Artis Henderson for wisdom and inspiration. I owe to her that this project even exists.

Thanks to Mary Hoffmann for a careful reading of the first draft and to Ginny Blanford for encouragement. And thanks to Valerie Duff for helpful guidance.

Thanks to my little Cape Coral writing group – especially our leader, Patricia Westbrook—and Lori Ruhl.

I am totally in debt to my family: to Tammy and Paul for letting me get their view on things and to Don for being as encouraging as a mortal can be.

CONTENTS

PROLOGUE

—Tammy, what do you dream about before you fall asleep?

—Nothing.

—What? Nothing?

—Right. I roll over and go to sleep.

—No princes, no magical frogs?

—What!? No. Sorry.

—Huh!

Well, there you are! Not everyone falls asleep imagining a better, more enchanted life. I find that surprising. As a little girl, I nodded off as a fairy in the sky. All the beings in my waking life were also up there, and at the moment I fell asleep I would magically draw them to me and with the ping of my wand, I would turn them into the stars of a constellation that was me, the fairy Margie.

I was roused from this dreamy megalomania when I was twelve. The brown-eyed, curly-haired, seventeen-year-old butcher's son delivered some meat to the house. I answered the door. "Here's the flank steak," he said.

That's all it took to pull me down from the starry night sky. The fairy Margie had pinged her last magical ping.

From that moment, my nightly vision was of marriage to the butcher's son. There was no courtship, no romance, no sex, come to think of it, just marriage and the production (immaculate, I guess) of triplets and multiple sets of twins, who nestled around me in awed adorableness under a flowery bower by the lily pond (sometimes a duck pond), listening to me read in the dappled light of one of the numerous atriums in our palace. Motherhood – this was my formative idyll.

I had a deck of Old Maid cards when I was a child. Woe to the player who was left with the baleful spinster at the end of the game. What could be worse than being an Old Maid? We made withering remarks about our own old maid teachers. No matter how excellent their classroom management or how engaging their teaching style or how dedicated they were to enlightening us about the meanings and spellings of the homonyms *there, their* and *they're,* they were still the most pitiable of humans. I marveled that they kept on living their sad lives, each a cautionary tale to me and to all girls.

Of the various doors before me in my young life, one hid the dread specter of spinsterhood. "Old Maid School Teacher" spelled doom for me, for me especially, because being a mother, more than anything else – more than career or romance or fame or money –was the counterpoise to the passage of time, the one thing that would give commitment, purpose, and love to the arc of my life.

But what was I worrying about? Everybody got married. The numbers were on my side. I mean, look how effortless it was. Like breathing air.

When she was grown and married, my daughter, Tammy (yes, the Tammy above is my daughter), accused me of not understanding how life is supposed to unfold. "Don't you get it, Mom? You get married and you have a baby." Really? Oh, that's brand-new information. That's one way to live your life, I guess. Never thought of that.

Some disturbed children bang their heads against the wall. When she was little Tammy hit her head hard with her hand repeatedly until it hurt, and she fought me with all her strength when I tried to stop her. Like mother, like daughter. I had spent my thirties banging my head against the singles scene of Manhattan. When you stop pounding your head, it feels good.

My mother's position was not far from my daughter's. "You took a hard path," my mother said, as though I had chosen my life, as though I had intentionally refused the course that she had taken– getting married young and having children. Hard path my foot. She must have known that it wasn't exactly a choice, that I didn't say to myself, "Here's an idea. I'll find a really messed up kid to raise." She must have known that taking in a foster child with issues instead of having babies with a partner committed to only me represented a compromise and not a preference.

Maybe it was hard, but once I did it, I never looked back. I was sustained by an optimistic, perhaps blind, belief in the power of my dogged persistence and the malleability of children when their environment responds to their needs. Raising Tammy alone actually made it easier. At least there was no one telling me how I ought to rear this troubled girl. I saw her with her previous foster family, wreaking havoc on a good marriage. I made mistakes every day, every hour, but there was no one else second-guessing me, no partner telling me I was too indulgent or too demanding, no heated discussions during which she could hear about how aberrant she was. There was just me and the cat, who decided to hate her on sight. Mushy Mushy would often look at me seeming to say, "Weren't we happy before?"

But no, I wasn't. Sorry, kitty.

So back then, I tucked away in the back of my mind the fail-safe that if I hadn't found a life partner by the time I was forty, then I would adopt. At thirty-five, I met a smart, fun guy named Warner. He had a PhD in physics (this impressed me), but he was severely allergic to cats. He had no business in an apartment with Mushy Mushy. I met him in October at an event listed under the rubric of Special/Social in the Village Voice. He was divorced with two adolescent sons who were on a trajectory toward the Ivies. He had a humorous overbite and a warm laugh. I saw that he was stumbling through life, but I didn't care. He said he loved me.

On December 13, he had an asthma attack, caused by the cat. I lived on Fifteenth Street, in Manhattan, right across from Friends Seminary, the school where I taught French. I came home during a free period and found him gasping to breathe. He couldn't talk. I called 911. When they came, they were demanding, even imperious. They told him to lie on the gurney. He tried, but he couldn't. As soon as he reclined even slightly, what little breathing power he had disappeared completely. He tried to show them that he had to kneel on the gurney. His desperation was intense, but they left him, saying, "Look, lady. He won't cooperate." They left. I stood there momentarily dumbstruck. What do you do when 911 fails you?

Propelled by terror, I raced to the lobby and told my doorman that my friend couldn't breathe. I must have conveyed my panic, because he ran out and stopped a police car. Four kind policemen filled my little apartment. They saw how critical the situation was and summoned the ambulance back. This time, the emergency men let Warner kneel on the gurney. They said they were going to Cabrini Hospital.

I think I went back and taught a class. I know I cancelled a parent conference. Then I went home and called Cabrini. They asked me who I was. I said that I was his girlfriend. They said maybe I would like to come in and talk. "You're scaring me," I said. "How is he?" They said that he was dead. The asthma attack had led to a heart attack in the ambulance.

I flailed about looking for some way to settle my shock. I wanted to console his sons. I wrote a story called Special/Social, took a professional day to visit the French classes in their uptown prep school, and gave the boys a copy. Much later, I learned that they were pursuing a lawsuit. I hope they got a lot of money.

I spent the next summer going to writers' conferences. At the one at Craigsville on Cape Cod, the teacher was a mystery writer named Harold Q. Masur. When he conferred with me about my story, he spent most of the time looking at my address. "Fifteenth Street?' he said. "Between what and what?"

"Second and Third."

"Oh, because I live on Twentieth."

I thought he was twenty years older than I was because of the blurb on the back of one of his books. It seemed a sure thing that this sweet old guy would give me a call, and he did, although he took his time and I had given up. I soon found that the book lied – he was thirty years older. I was thirty-six and he was sixty-six. He had been a lawyer who tried to put out a shingle when he came back from World War II but had the insoluble problem that he didn't have it in him to send out bills.

All his life, Hal explained to himself that he hadn't married because he was worried about money. He invested half of every royalty check he received and lived a frugal existence. If you do that all your life, a moment comes when you don't have to worry about money any more. He looked at me and was at a loss to understand what the problem was. "Face it, Hal. You are the very definition of a confirmed bachelor."

It was a comfortable thing for me. He cooked for me every night and made sure he had plenty of material to keep me laughing. He could admit to being "crazy about" me, but I'm pretty sure the word love gave him vertigo. For years, he emceed the Mystery Writers of America Annual Awards. "No one can quiet a crowd like me." He was a guy who "had a million of them." Jokes, that is. He had been a stand-up comic at the resorts of the Borsht Belt – also a tennis pro and general factotum.

"Marge. Why do you call yourself Marge?"

"Uh, it's my name. Why do you call yourself Hal?"

"No, no. You're not a Marge. You're a Maggie. "

I explained to him that I was pushing forty, and I had a strong desire to have kids. I had to see other people.

"First whatshisname croaks on you and then me. Poor Maggie."

But when I met a guy named Jim, Hal had a nightmare that Jim was breaking through the walls of his bedroom. He took a little break from me. After Jim, there was Greg. Jim drank. Quite a bit. Greg wanted to make love in public places – airplanes, the backseat of taxis (never mind that my mother was sitting on the other side of me). I was forming the theory that normal men had long since been beamed up to another planet.

Hal resumed cooking for me. I wept over the dead end my life had become.

"Jeez, "he said. "No more water works. I don't have the Kleenex budget for it."

I went to an adoption agency. The social worker asked me what church I attended.

"None."

"None?" She shook her head slowly and uttered a pessimistic tsk-tsk. "You have some chance of adopting a child."

I gathered that she meant 'no chance at all.' It occurred to me to quickly convert to some mainstream religion, but I figured I'd best be straight with her. "Well, I don't particularly believe in anything."

"Come on. You must believe in something. Everybody believes in something."

"Well, yes, of course." My brain was straining; it finally came up with, "I believe it's great that we have four seasons."

"Ah ha," she said. "You're a Unitarian."

I said I'd give it a try.

I took a required course in parenting. A woman who had adopted two little Korean boys told of how they had dragged their beds down the stairs in the middle of the night planning to take them back home to their mother in Korea. It seemed to me that if we cared about kids, we would subsidize the Korean mother. Better to take in kids with dead or incarcerated parents.

I looked through the thick volumes with thousands of pages of children waiting for a home. Most were at least ten years old. A few were in their teens. Want to have your heart broken? Just look at all those sad kids. I thought I might as well take one. Their need for a home seemed to outweigh my desire to raise a younger child. What I wished for was a four-year old girl so that she wouldn't already be completely formed, yet would still be able to attend school while I worked.

In the summer of 1982, when I was forty-two years old, I did a trial run at mothering. There was a Cambodian refugee at Friends, who was struggling with English. I offered to take her for a month or so in the summer. Her mother and stepfather had survived the holocaust there, but all of her siblings had perished. Her parents agreed that a visit with me would benefit Sroeun.

She looked like one of Gauguin's Polynesian beauties come to life. I would guess she was about fifteen.

She told me it was her birthday. I later discovered that she always told people it was her birthday. Clever girl. I gave her five dollars, which she spent on five meat shish kabobs a vendor was selling at Battery Park. For the years of the Cambodian tragedy, all she had eaten was rice. She still craved meat.

My niece and nephew, Becky and Andy, came over from New Jersey to help me show Sroeun the sights of New York. We went to the top of the old World Trade Center where she had a panic attack when we hopped on an escalator. I called back to her, "Just stay there – we'll get you." A Chinese family pulled her out of the pedestrian stream as Andy ran back up the down escalator. She had never seen an escalator before.

Sroeun told me that her mother wanted me to come visit them in Brooklyn. Their basement apartment, overflowing with refugees, was furnished with mismatched, cast off chairs they had picked up off the street. No one spoke English, but they overwhelmed me with hospitality, offering me the chair with the most intact upholstery and plying me with orange soda and Cheetos. They tried to communicate with gestures and a few random words of English. I finally realized that they were describing their mad dash through the forest of land mines between Cambodia and Thailand. Sroeun said, "People blow up."

I looked at her mother, who had lost child after child, and saw a face drained of all life. Sroeun told me that when her last little brother was killed, "Oh my mom, she cry and she cry."

I took Sroeun to the Metropolitan Museum, thinking she might enjoy looking at some of the Asian artifacts. As I whisked her through the European paintings, she suddenly stopped. Her hand was on her heart. Her mouth was open and she was panting.

"What is it, Sroeun?" I asked.

Her eyes scanned the gallery full of old masters. "It's so good!" she finally managed.

It had never occurred to me that this wealth of art would reach her.

"Well, why don't we look at these, then?" I said.

She examined the works up close and then from a little distance. The only sentence she uttered in this rapt state was, "Someone did these. Oh."

So this girl, whose childhood was littered with carnage and grief, glimpsed the miracle of what our species can do.

When she had to go home, I told Hal that looking after Sroeun had really made me happy. That's when he said, "I know this dame – I did a closing for her. She has a half-brother or something who's in jail and his kids are up for grabs. There's a little girl who's about four. Maybe you could get her."

That's how I heard of my Tammy.

PART I
1983-1988

1

THREE GOOD FAIRIES

Three strangers made it happen. The first of these good fairies was Shaunie. Everyone called Hal's client Shaunie, although her name was Katherine, because her maiden name was Shaughnessy. She grew up in Philadelphia in the forties and then, when she was in high school, she had an opportunity to participate in a year-long program in New York City.

Feeling very independent, she didn't see much of her parents that year. Her sister and brother were also on their own, and for much of her time in New York, she was out of touch with her family.

Toward the end of this year, in direct opposition to all she knew about them, her parents divorced, and her mother disappeared from her life. They were devout Catholics, so this break in what had seemed an eternal marriage was a bewildering shock. When Shaunie questioned her father, all she got was rage against her mother. He refused to give his children any information that would help them understand what went wrong and banished their mother from their lives, forbidding them to say one word about her. History was rewritten with the mother excised. Shaunie, her brother, and sister were left with a mystery.

Nonetheless, Shaunie was an independent soul and turned to her new life as a young adult with all her energy. She married, had a son and a daughter, made a great deal of money in Manhattan real estate, divorced, and made some more money.

Hal knew her socially, and when she purchased another rental property, she asked if he would dust off his attorney skills and do the closing. That's when he heard about the little girl, Tammy.

Hal arranged for us to have dinner with Shaunie. The "dame" turned out to be a charming talker with a melodic voice and a ready laugh. I guessed she was about a decade older than I was and though she was not very tall, she was an imposing presence. A dealmaker, she was in the habit of winning in negotiations and court cases. I hoped she would be on my side; I was sure her other side was no place to be.

In our cozy booth, in a tiny Fifth Avenue restaurant, Shaunie pulled out pictures of her four nephews and niece. The little girl stared out at me through angry eyes and an aggressive scowl. She was a very tiny four-year-old. Three of the brothers were older and another was only three.

"None of them are very bright," Shaunie said, laughing. "I think the little girl might be the brightest, but what a temper. We're in a store in this picture. I was buying her some new clothes when, oh my God, she had such a tantrum I thought I'd have a lawsuit from the store. Small but dangerous."

I looked at the picture carefully and could see the curtain of a dressing room in the background. Tammy looked ready for a rumble. If she could channel this fight, maybe she could turn out like her aunt.

So. Not bright with a dangerous temper. Sounded promising.

But here was my thought. She was only four. She had had a hard life. She needed a home. Sure, I had heard horror stories. A colleague had taken in a child who wandered around the home after all were asleep looking at his new family with homicidal rage. My colleague would wake up in the night to see a face that made her fear for her life and the life of her other child. When she awakened one night to find this child with a knife in his hand, she had to find him another placement. But four, I reasoned, is a bit young to attempt murder, isn't it? Tammy didn't look dangerous to me. She looked traumatized, and I was banking on my own patience.

Shaunie already had little Martin, age three, and Matthew, age six, living in her home. She wanted to help me get Tammy.

"Here's what happened," she said. "My phone rings out of the blue, and this guy says, 'Hello, this is your brother, Martin Shaughnessy.'

"'Whoa, whoa, whoa,' I say. 'I have a brother and his name isn't Martin, and he is certainly not you.'

"'Please, don't hang up. We do have the same mother. I have five kids and I need help.'

"I'm cleaning up how he spoke—he sounded like a hayseed. Anyway, I thought it was some kind of scam to get money out of me. So I called my sister to see if this made any sense to her. She allowed that she had been around when Mom left and that something she overheard made her think that Mom might be pregnant – and not by Dad.

"When she said that, some things began to make sense. No wonder my father was so angry. So I realized that it was possible that this guy could be that baby."

A long-lost baby brother produced by an illicit affair. Oh, and who had an abandoned girl-child of his own who was just the age of child I wanted to raise. I wouldn't put this in a work of fiction.

"Wow," I said. "Sounds like an episode of *The Young and the Restless*."

"And how!" she said. "Anyway, once I was convinced that he was a half-brother, I just felt I had to help. He and his I-don't-know-what but I'm pretty sure not his wife were living in Miami in utter squalor with the five kids. I couldn't walk away. I went down there, set them up in a decent apartment, saw to it that Martin had a job, and then came back. So I tried. But no sooner was I back in New York than Martin wound up in jail for fraud – I don't know what he did – and all the kids were in foster care. I don't know what Bonnie, the mom, was up to, but the caseworker said it was 'near a motel' and 'pretty sleazy.' You draw your own conclusions."

"So this guy, this half-brother, his last name was the same as yours?" I asked.

"Oh, it's quite weird that his name was Shaughnessy, after all, he was someone else's kid, but at the time he was born, Mom was still married to Dad, so that's how it went down on the birth certificate."

Shaunie promised to get in touch with HRS (Health and Rehabilitative Services, now called Department of Children and Families). Two days later she called me.

"I said I had a friend who would take the little girl. They said something to the effect of, 'Are you kidding? We would have to go through the Interstate Compact.' Apparently, that involved depleting the forests of Canada to do the paper work. So I tried a new tack; I said I had a cousin who would take the girl. Well they went for that, so you're my cousin. 'Family placement.'"

"Oh God. You are too much! How are we going to pull this off?" I had been such a good girl all my life! What, commit fraud myself?

"First, I'm telling you, I will not lie under oath. No way. It's all over if they swear me in," she said. "But that won't happen. Tell me some names in your family."

"Well, my mother's name was McGinnis."

"No kidding. Our great family friends in Philly were McGinnises. But we need to be relatives. My mother's maiden name was Harris."

"Oh wow, that's funny."

"What?"

"My grandmother's maiden name was Harris."

"That's it then."

The co-conspirators got together at her house to make sure we had our stories straight. I met Matt and little Martin, the brothers, who showed a talent for making car noises. "Vrmm vrmm," came at me from unexpected angles as Shaunie and I knitted together our families. Matt, eager to please, repeatedly inquired, "Am I doing it right, Aunt Shaunie?" The dates worked out well enough for an aunt-niece relationship between my grandmother and her mother. Shaunie had her mother's birth certificate and I had a newspaper notice of my grandmother's marriage. This would make us distant relations, but that was all we needed.

As it turned out, it never came up for us to say anything more. No one ever asked me if Shaunie was really my cousin.

I wrote to HRS and filled out forms. A social worker had to do a home study. An extremely untidy housekeeper, I was in trepidation of what I imagined would be a white glove test. I had moved from the studio apartment across the street from the school to a one-bedroom in Stuyvesant Town. What if there was a requirement for a separate bedroom for the child? A lot of worry for nothing. Instead of a prissy lady, I got a very young lanky black man, whose mind was not on my clutter or lack of space.

As soon as he came in, he asked for a glass of water. He said he just came from a case where a stepfather had beaten a two-year-old to death in Central Park. He slumped on my sofa, fighting the tears as he said, "I didn't get there in time." I wept with him. What a dreadful job! It seemed to me he was too sensitive to last very long. Either that or he'd have to find a compartment for his emotions and shut down the very qualities that brought him to helping people. I looked in *The Times* for this story but it wasn't there. I wondered if such horrors passed for ordinary in the world of foster care.

Shaunie found out the name and number of Tammy's foster family. Now it was time to jump through some hoops to bring little Tammy home.

The second good fairy was Foree. Christmas break was my first chance to meet Tammy. I wanted to take her with me to my parents' in Fort Myers, but Foree, Tammy's foster mother, preferred for me to visit them in Miami for a few days before Christmas. Maybe she thought I wouldn't like Tammy or that she wouldn't like me. Turns out she was concerned about how many heads I had.

Eagerly anticipating meeting Tammy, I stepped out of the airport into the muggy, midwinter warmth of Florida. Foree picked me up, and then instead of driving me to her home, wound her way through the complicated infrastructure of Miami to a coffee house. I nervously wondered what this new holdup was all about. Would I ever meet this child?

Foree chatted pleasantly as I anxiously tried to be civil. Tall and unpretentious, she dressed like a boy and seemed completely comfortable in her skin. She impressed the world inadvertently—with the force of her conversation, strewn with nuggets of wit and wisdom. She had fostered a couple of babies before she took Tammy. "I had to know if you had three heads," she said as we ordered coffee. Now, all these years later, I see her point. She didn't know me.

With its dark paneling and well-worn bar, the coffee shop looked like a former Irish pub. Foree led me to a booth. Another mother and her Down syndrome adolescent son, friends of Foree, joined us. I was with the regulars. "You'll love Tammy," said the mother. If I ever meet her, I thought.

"That's for sure," Foree said. "I send her and my daughter Roxana to the Blue Bird Preschool. Tammy came home the other day with a note pinned to her. 'She just needs love. She'll be fine.'"

The boy's mother said that he was a joy. They had told her that he couldn't achieve, and now he was succeeding in eighth grade math. "So there. I'm proud of you, Sweetie."

"Wow," I said. "That's quite an accomplishment. Eighth grade math. Good for you!"

The cherub face lit up.

"Head count," said Foree, as she took her last sip. "She only has one. Let's get going."

Roxana, and Tammy were sitting at a little child table when we came in.

"Say hello to Aunt Margie," said Foree. Two adorable heads looked up. One said, "Hello, Aunt Margie." The other said, "Hewo an ma-ee." Roxana was relaxed and smiling, a child who had been securely loved her whole life; Tammy's face was strained and worried. Her dirty blond hair hung in wispy strands.

Love at first sight in French is *le coup de foudre*, being struck by lightning. One look at Tammy and Thor's bolt got me where I live. Though oh-so-needy, she squared her shoulders tough-girl style, seeming to say, "Don't think of me as a victim. I have a say in things." As her green eyes fixed on me, I was stunned by her fragility. This was my baby. Already. A song began to loop in my head. "You are the one that I always dreamed of."

Eager to know Tammy, I sat in an armchair holding some books that Jane, the kindergarten teacher at Friends, had loaned me. "Come on, Tammy, let's look at some books." She sat on my lap, happy to have captivated the attention of this visitor. "What's this?" I asked, pointing to the picture of a rake. She didn't know. Oh well, I thought, she has lived her whole life in Florida. They don't have fall. Later I asked Roxana, who was only three, and she said, "That's a rake. You use it to rake leaves."

Tammy accidentally knocked my water glass off a table and when it broke, she was stricken with distress. The shattered glass and the spilled water alarmed her beyond measure. She wailed and cried wet tears as Foree cleaned it up, soothingly repeating, "It's okay." She's motivated, I thought.

We took to the coloring book I had brought and the friendly smell of Crayolas. This is what I wanted to do – color with a little girl. "I like blue. What about you?"

"BWACK."

Foree called us to the table for lunch. There were five of us – the two girls, Foree, her husband Lyle, and me. Foree said grace, giving thanks for the food, and then asked for a blessing and a new carburetor. "Amen."

"What is the matter with you?" said Lyle. "You don't pray for specific things like carburetors."

"You don't, huh," she said. "Where do you think you came from?"

The next day we went to the foster home of Tammy's second oldest brother, Steven. I had already met him at Shaunie's, and had to agree with her pronouncement—"Drop dead gorgeous." Steven lived in a home filled with foster children. At that moment, he was the only white inhabitant. Tammy had lived there too the year before. The house was in Liberty City, an area that had suffered riots in the past, and still looked a little sketchy.

The foster mother had rules and could only cope with compliant children. The mother told me Tammy was "just too much." The kids played out back. If they wanted to come back in, they had to knock and say, "Mother may I please" before entering or getting so much as a sip of water. I saw why Tammy hadn't lasted.

"Why don't you buy him shoes," said Foree. "They always need shoes." We went off to the mall and a beaming Steven came away with cowboy boots

Tammy was a chatterbox. Unfortunately, I couldn't understand a thing she said. "Do you understand her, Steven?"

"Not usually."

Foree told me what she knew about Tammy's rocky history. This placement with Foree and Lyle was her fifth. We surmised that she was with her biological mother until her father's incarceration a year and a half earlier when she and her four brothers were removed from their biological family. One family rejected her because she soiled her pants on a camping trip. There was at least one other placement in addition to the one with Steven, but Foree had no idea what happened there. All of this moving around must have taken place since her third birthday, though who knows? She might have been in and out of foster care during her first three years. No one at HRS had the slightest inclination to fill me in.

I went back to New York with a sense of desperation. In my mind, Tammy was already my child. I was obsessed with repairing her basic trust, so damaged by a life rife with upheavals. Why was she so afraid when she broke the glass? She must have been punished harshly in one of those placements.

The longing to bring her home would jolt me at unexpected times, and I would pace about my apartment, slapping walls and furniture. She needed to be here. She needed constant, permanent love. The song kept playing in my mind. "I saw your face and that's the last I've seen of my heart." I railed against HRS for dragging their feet. She was not in speech therapy, and they were to blame. They were supposed to be her advocates. If anyone was Maleficent, Mistress of Evil, it was HRS. I had finished all the paperwork and the home-study in November. During December, January, February, and March I heard nothing from them. What were they waiting for? Wasn't it their job to get foster children into a settled placement?

By day, it was their fault. By night, it was mine. I couldn't sleep; over and over, my mind replayed the same thoughts. I was weak. I didn't know how to push against the system. Here was a cast-off child. Nobody wanted her. Yet I failed to persuade them to act. I was no match for the logjam. Suffering from my powerlessness to bring her home to me, when I finally nodded off, I had nightmares.

During my spring break, I brought Tammy to Fort Myers for nearly two weeks. Foree and I both tried to clear this with HRS, but since they weren't responding to either one of us, we just went ahead. Tammy had turned five in February, but she seemed just as tiny. I gave her gum so her ears wouldn't pop on the short hop from Miami to Fort Myers.

On the plane I asked, "Where's your gum?"

She looked worried. "Did you swallow it?" I laughed. Then she laughed too. A laugh of relief. My parents picked us up, and though we couldn't understand her, she seemed to understand us. In the car, she began to sing. Through the garbled consonants, we made out that she was singing, "Praise Him, Praise Him, all ye little children."

"Can you beat that," said my father, a Lutheran minister.

"This one will do," said my mother.

In the condo, Tammy found a drawer in the buffet, with about a dozen candles formed to look like children choristers. She lined them up and began giving them instruction. "Woo do dis" and "Woo do dat." The little figures constantly regrouped to do her bidding. She was occupied for hours. At the end of a session the buffet top was thick with wax.

In the evening, she played with a rag doll named Girl and a stuffed panda named Panda. For years, Girl was her alter ego. Tammy heard me mention this to people, and she would say, "This is Girl. Her last name is Allereego."

Foree said that her one requirement was that I have a rocking chair. My parents had one, and at night I rocked her, singing lullabies by the hour. "Sleep my child," "Hush my dear," "Dreamland opens here," tumbled out of some corner of my memory.

As Tammy nodded off, I sang the tune stuck in my head. "You are the one that I always dreamed of." But I was still Aunt Marge, and as far as she knew she was just a cherished niece. I was alone in limbo.

My brother and his family were coming for Easter. We looked through photo albums so that Tammy would know Uncle Joe, Aunt Sharon, Andy and Becky. The albums seized her attention. She considered the pictures, with care, squinting to check the fine details. Suddenly she began to wail. She wanted to throw the albums on the floor. She seemed dangerously near to ripping out pages.

"Tammy. Tammy, what's the matter?"

"Where Ca'y?"

"Oh, my God. You're right."

My mother came running in. "What's the matter with her?"

"She's upset because her picture isn't in the album. Tammy, listen Honey, you're right. Your picture isn't in there yet. Don't worry, Sweetie. We'll take pictures of you and put them in."

She blotted her face against my leg and cried her eyes out.

"Poor baby," said Mom.

My niece Becky had just turned ten, so I took Tammy shopping at Edison Mall to buy a gift. We found a necklace, had it gift-wrapped, and headed back to the car. As we passed the food court, we heard music. At a store that sold musical instruments, someone was playing jaunty tunes on an electric organ. Tammy broke away from me and started to dance. She lost herself in the music. With no self-consciousness, this tiny child twirled, charming the crowd. Arms up and head up, she was in her own personal trance. She swayed. She rocked. When the music stopped, applause broke out. A lady said to me, "She is so adorable." Then she turned to Tammy and said, "What's your name, Honey?"

"Ca'y," she said.

"Cammy," said the lady.

"No," said Tammy with frustration and anger. "Ca'y."

"Tammy," I said.

"Oh TAMMY," said the lady. "Well Tammy, you are a very beautiful dancer."

We no sooner got back to the condo than my brother and company showed up. Tammy ran to get Becky's present and before I could stop her, tore away the wrapping paper, opened the box, pulled out the string of beads and handed them to Becky, who laughed and thanked her profusely. Twelve-year-old Andy picked her up and swung her onto his shoulders. She squealed and grabbed his head for dear life.

Photos of the next days are numerous: Tammy, Andy and Becky in the pool, Becky and Tammy dying Easter Eggs, Tammy helping Andy and Becky play shuffleboard. The photo album would be stuffed with pictures of Tammy.

On Saturday night Sharon said, "What are we thinking? We don't have our Easter baskets together." Sharon and I hurried to the supermarket to pick up the chocolate eggs and bunnies. "This is a must," Sharon said as she threw bubble gum into our cart. I wasn't too sure. I figured Tammy would swallow it again. But Sharon had a decade of experience. I was feeling the elation of a rookie. As it turned out, the bubble gum was the one thing in Tammy's basket that she was excited about.

What she really loved was the Easter egg hunt at the Lutheran church. She flew around the little garden in her new pink dress. The angelic sprite would have killed for a purple egg.

Her hair was streaked with gold from all the sun time in the pool. It seemed to me that a bit of the strain in her face had melted. I flew back to New York while she stayed with my parents until Foree, Lyle, and Roxana picked her up on the way back from a trip to Tampa. My mother told me that Foree brought her a Teddy bear. So now Girl and Panda had a new friend—Bear.

The third good fairy was Ronald Reagan. When I got back, I was faced with the reality that I was nowhere nearer getting custody of her. My nights were again sleepless. I wrote her father in jail. He wrote back in illiterate but expressive prose, supporting me. "Them kids never messed up like that when they was with me." I told him I would take care of her and see that she got the services she needed. Since HRS stopped taking my calls, I wrote them on any pretext. The panicky feeling that I was not doing enough clung to me. I wrote to Senator Moynihan, making my case that Tammy needed the security of a permanent home lickity split. Shaunie wrote to Ronald Reagan.

"Are you kidding, Shaunie? What will the President do?"

"You'd be surprised. You always have to go to the top."

Through my parents, I heard about a lawyer in Miami – Kendall Coffey. Now I see him on TV from time to time as a legal expert. He spoke with me and then called HRS. The pressure from Senator Moynihan's office had only served to enrage them. Mr. Coffey advised me to back off. They would do the paper work in their own time.

April went by and now we were well into May. As I was grading papers in the Friends Seminary Faculty Lounge, the phone rang. "It's for you, Marge." Then *sotto voce,* "It's the White House."

"Hello?"

"Yes, this is the White House calling. We are responding to the letter we received about your difficulty with the Miami HRS office."

"Yes." Oh my God, oh my God. "Oh yes. Thank you so much for calling. Here's the situation. I think that all the parties involved agree that I should get this child, Tammy Shaughnessy, but there is this obstacle of the paper work."

"Since October, they have failed to do the paper work?"

"That's right."

"Okay. Well, why don't we give them a little goose? I think it would be reasonable for them to do the paper work by Tuesday or lose their federal funding. How does that sound?"

"Oh, reasonable. Very reasonable. Thank you so much." Then for no apparent reason I added, "My brother's a Republican."

I imagined the caseworker getting the call and felt a brief pang of pity for her. I had better start making my apartment kid friendly.

2
MOM NUMBER THREE

Foree came to visit me with Roxana and Tammy at the beginning of June, just as my school let out. Since Stuyvesant Town did not permit air-conditioning at that time, my apartment was sweltering. We went down to the tip of Manhattan and took the Staten Island Ferry, just for the cool breeze and the stunning views of the city.

Foree chased after Roxana, who could not resist the spectacle of the ferry's wake, while Tammy sat with me on a bench, looking out over the water. I thought about my good fortune that Foree was Tammy's foster mother. In contrast to the coldness of the obstructionist bureaucracy, Foree sought to ensure that Tammy had the best chance possible. She was a one-person social service agency, checking me out before I saw Tammy, insisting that the first visit be in Miami in her home, suggesting I buy the children shoes so she could see if I really wanted to help them, letting me take Tammy to Fort Myers, and now bringing Tammy to stay with me for three weeks without the knowledge or permission of HRS.

The next day, Foree gave her blessing to my newest purchase, a rocking chair. Then she and Roxana left Tammy with me until the court date on July 3rd.

Tammy came in time to begin the three-week summer camp program Friends Seminary holds every June. Of course it was my cherished dream that Tammy go to my school as a kindergartener in the fall. Jane, the longtime teacher of the class of four and five year olds, was also working with this age in the June program. She would have a chance to assess whether this would work. Tammy and I could have a dress rehearsal for what was to come.

As my apartment had only one bedroom, I got a member of the art department, who taught woodworking, to build a loft in the dining area. It was four feet high below and above. The bottom level was for sleeping and the top, accessed by a little ladder, was for playing. From the kitchen, I could keep an eye on Tammy's play "upstairs." She loved to line up all her stuffed animals, with Girl, Panda, and Bear in starring roles, and talk to them endlessly, just as she had the wax choristers. In the evening, I would crawl up there and sit on the carpeted floor and read to her.

One morning, a week or so after she arrived, I went into the bathroom and saw that the kitty litter box was full of water, the disgusting little turds floating on top. The water was overflowing. We were on the tenth floor. Oh Lord, what if the water was seeping through to the downstairs neighbors? Oh no. What was she thinking?

"Oh my God, Tammy! Tammy, are you kidding me? Tammy, come here right now. What happened here?"

She came in, saw the evidence of her crime, and began to scream and to hit me. "Wait a minute here. You don't get to scream. You made a big mess. I should be screaming." Oh man, I was getting pummeled. Had she heard somewhere that the best defense was a good offence? Her thirty-five pounds must have been pure muscle. I tried to catch her arms and pin them to her body. She landed me a good one in the stomach.

"You stop this. Stop this right now."

If you'd asked me a week before if I was capable of hitting a child, I would have said, "No." I knew the party line. All they learn from that is that it's all right to hit.

Now I reached around and caught her a glancing blow to her rear end. She let out a shriek that would wake the dead. I gave her another thump to the rear. I held her arms to her body and looked her in the eyes.

"Did you do this by mistake or on purpose?"

"On purpose."

"You did this on purpose?" I screamed, outraged.

"By mistake. By mistake."

She stalked off to cry at the top of her lungs and whack her head with her hands.

Well, I thought, at least she's had a vocabulary lesson. Now she knows that the best answer is always "by mistake, not on purpose."

Every day I took her to one of the playgrounds of Stuyvesant Town where they had big showers for the kids to frolic in. Tammy gravitated to any black children who might be there. The Liberty City experience had brought about the most non-racist child I had seen.

She was never ready to leave the playground. There was always a tantrum. These outbursts were frequent, frenzied and loud. My strategy (maybe a bit risky, but it was all I could think of) was to walk out of the playground, head for home and never look back. Pretty soon a little girl would be at my side, too terrified of abandonment to continue her fit.

Trips to the supermarket were no better. There was no good time to go through the checkout line either. Though she couldn't read, I gave her the shopping list, and come hell or high water, we were not diverting from it even if I'd accidentally omitted much needed milk. When we got to the moment of truth, the conveyor belt next to the enticing candy display, I let her scream. "What's the matter with her?" asked the lady behind me.

"She wants candy, but it's not on the list."

"Well, then, stick to your guns, Honey!"

Tammy loved the June program, and since school was out for me, I could volunteer to chaperone school trips. I went with the group to the Staten Island Zoo and later to the beach. Clearly, Tammy was not on a level with everyone else either verbally or socially. She managed to alienate the other little girls by throwing sand at their faces. I cringed when I overheard other children grousing about her. "Tammy, oh I hate her." "Me too, I HATE her SO much."

The second weekend, my dear friends Donna and Bob were getting married at a lovely setting, an elegant private school situated on the bank of the Hudson, about an hour away. This was the first time I needed a babysitter and luckily my parents were visiting my brother in Princeton and would come to the city to stay with her. Unluckily, at the last minute my mother came down with a case of shingles. She didn't know what she had, but she knew she was in pain and covered with hives. She felt that she had to get back to Florida to see her doctor.

When I went to the school to pick Tammy up the day before the wedding, I asked Jane who could babysit her. She recommended a rising senior who had known Tammy these two weeks. She was willing to take care of Tammy, but I was beside myself with anxiety. How would she handle one of those fierce outbursts? I felt that Tammy was so special and so fragile that no one besides me could deal with her. The baby sitter, Kim, was a mature seventeen-year-old, certainly calmer than I. "Don't worry," she said. "I already know her. She'll be fine."

The ceremony was outside with the river in the background. Donna's frail and ailing father had the joy of walking her down the aisle. Bob in his white yarmulke and Donna in her subtly hooped long dress stood under the white trellis, draped with flower garlands. The wedding was so beautiful that it swept me along. At the reception, Donna handed me the video camera and commissioned me to interview the guests. A band was playing, the setting was elegant, and food and wine were abundant. It was a historic event in the life of our little group. We called ourselves "the family we chose."

Eventually though, I began to succumb to worry. I went out and looked at the river. Donna's brother, whom I barely knew, came out to talk with me. I told him how fragile Tammy was, how often her behavior was disturbed. I told him about how agitated I felt, wondering if the baby sitter could handle her. He had raised two children. He listened to me patiently, and then he made a stab at comforting me. He said, "You know, she isn't really all that fragile. She's made it this far. Kids are basically resilient."

I felt reassured, but I still got into the first car going back to the city. She was fine, of course. She loved Kim. She had had fun. I had my first taste of life as a worrywart.

—What do you remember about going to court when you were five?

—Nothing.

—You told me about a pink dress.

—Yeah but that wasn't when we went to court.

—When was it?

—I don't know when it was. I just remember a pink flowery satiny dress with a matching hairband and I hated it.

—I think you had it for Easter and then wore it again for the court date.

—I only remember wearing that hideous thing once.

—What's your objection to a pink dress?

—It's pink. I do black, not pink. I still don't do pink. I've never done pink.

Tammy and I flew to Miami for the court date. We stayed with Foree, Lyle, and Roxana. Foree drove Tammy, looking adorable in her pink smocked Easter dress and headband, and me to the courthouse.

I was a little afraid of encountering the caseworker who had received the call from the White House, but naturally she had to be there. She turned out to be a small bedraggled woman, stooped over carrying her great sheaf of papers. I guessed she was in her forties and burned out from all she had seen and couldn't do.

Back in the late fall when she was taking my calls, this caseworker dismissed me saying that she had—what was it?—two hundred cases maybe.

I didn't pay attention since I was interested in only one. I figured that she should clear the decks of this one and then take care of the other hundred ninety-nine. She probably figured that Tammy was in a good home, so why not put me on a back burner.

She greeted me perfunctorily and seemed genuinely happy to see Foree. A foster mother she could count on was undoubtedly rare and prized. Foree poked her on the arm and said, "What do you say when this is over we go out and meet a couple of sailors?" For a fleeting moment, the dour earnestness gave way to a smile.

In the back of the courtroom, we ran into a woman who was pretty in exactly the same ways as Tammy, so similar in features and hair that I immediately knew she was the biological mother. Dressed in faded jeans and flipflops, Bonnie Jackson looked out of step with the court's decorum. Her expression was marked with so much anxiety that I remembered with guilt laughing at her along with my colleagues in the faculty room and labeling her trailer trash. We had been wrong; she was a tragic figure; she had given birth to eight babies, none of whom were in her life.

Imagining all she had suffered, I felt kindly disposed toward her though I was afraid of her, too, of what she could do if she found a sugar daddy, of how she could rip this child from me, of how precarious she made my life with Tammy. But I also recognized that she was on a downhill path where there was little chance of her survival once her looks were gone. I had a pang of sorrow, thinking that I wished I had been her mother so I could have helped her when she needed help the way I was going to help Tammy, the way I would alter Tammy's path so that she did not have to become her mother.

Later I learned that Bonnie had trouble with school. Her one saving grace was baton twirling. Her own mother struggled to make ends meet as a waitress; she was single with another child as well. This left her little energy to rein in a daughter whose only comfort was her flair for attracting men. As a teen, Bonnie had three babies, all of whom were placed for adoption. I looked into this lovely but oh-so-strained face and wondered how she could endure parting with baby after baby. It was unfathomable to me that no one stepped in to see to it that she had the pill. An aunt of hers from Alabama told me that those first three children were two boys and a girl, and the girl looked just like Tammy.

Bonnie became a cocaine user. As a young adult, she had five more children with Martin Shaughnessy. I wished I knew what effect cocaine would have on a developing fetus. I had heard that alcohol could wreak havoc in utero, and it seemed more than likely that she'd had a drink or two during her pregnancies. I supposed that my belief in the power of environment might face some tough obstacles. But I quickly dismissed this thought because it already didn't matter. Tammy was my child. Does it matter when a birth child comes with imperfections?

"Hi Bonnie, I'm Marge Gonzalez."

"Hay," she said with a southern drawl. "Thank you for taking care of Tammy. I can't do it right now. I'm gonna try to get things worked out. Then I'll come pick her up and the four boys."

"Okay," I said, with a sharp intake of breath, the air in the room suddenly seeming too thin. If they had to bring in a wise judge like Solomon someday, I worried that I would be the first to blink. Would I yield to keep the child from being torn apart, or would I stand my ground, knowing that I had greater strength in every way except heredity?

The caseworker pulled me aside. "Don't worry. There's not a chance in the world that she will get any of her kids back."

I wished I had it in writing.

Foree, Bonnie, and I sat on a bench at the back of the courtroom. Tammy, in her pink Easter dress, looked at each of us, one after the other, three mommies in a row. She made a sound like "Eh-eh-eh," while waving her hands up and down in front of each of us. She was standing, and the only place to sit was on one of these three laps. Like the little ball on a roulette wheel, she teased. Which would she choose?

Something in her wanted to choose each one. She stopped in front of Foree. Here was the loving mother who had nurtured her for months. Foree had prepared her kindly and steadily for a separation. I think Tammy also felt that as much as Foree loved her, as much as Foree would try to shield her from this feeling, she would always play second fiddle to Roxana. Still, she stood a while, looking at Foree and making her sound and then moved on.

She looked at Bonnie and couldn't help feeling the tug of shared DNA. She wanted Bonnie as one wants an old lover who said goodbye first. But like that rejected lover, she was angry with Bonnie. A few months later she said to me in the most wrenchingly heartbroken of tones, "I wuved her so much, and see sai' see pick me up and see di'in. See di'in pick me up." All those foster homes where Tammy languished waiting for this mother who never came.

Tammy stopped in front of me and stretched out her arms, asking to be picked up. I put her on my lap. Foree leaned over and whispered, "Looks like you win." True. The little roulette ball landed in my lap. But then, she knew what was coming; the wheel was rigged.

"All rise."

The judge, a middle-aged man came in. "We are here regarding the foster placement of the child Tammy Lynn Shaughnessy."

The caseworker gave her report, recommending that Tammy be placed with me. I offered up a little thank you to Ronald Reagan.

"That okay with you, Ms. Jackson?"

"Yes, Sir. I can't take care of her right now."

He looked at Tammy and me and asked. "This okay with you Tammy?"

No answer. Too busy playing with my earring.

Then it was over. I had official custody of Tammy. She looked at me and said, "Mommy!" There should have been confetti and fireworks.

As fast as that, Foree became "Aunt Foree."

3

HOW TO FIX A DISTURBED CHILD

FAMILY AND PLACE

After lunch, we packed up her things, said goodbye to Foree, Lyle, and Roxana, promised to come visit, and took off across Alligator Alley to Fort Myers to spend some time with Tammy's newly official grandparents. She fell asleep in the back seat as I drove through the monotonous landscape, punctuated occasionally by ibises on the wing or wading in the long roadside swales.

I felt the immense relief of having finally won the struggle to get this little girl. Now I could help her. Now I could offer her my family. Now I could get her into emotional therapy and speech therapy. She could make my school her own. Here it was at last. I could claim the title of *mother.* Though I was legally only her foster mother, I knew in my bones that her placement with me was final. I could wait out the slow-moving bureaucracy that would eventually have to surrender her for adoption.

Tammy woke up when we turned north at Naples. I heard her warning Girl to behave herself.

When we got to their condo, two beaming septuagenarians greeted us at the door. Mom scooped Tammy up and said, "Hey, Tammy, how's our pretty little granddaughter?"

"Good," said Tammy as she squirmed to the floor and headed to the drawer with the wax candle choristers.

"I haven't had a chance to shop for dinner," said Mom. "We were waiting for you. Let's go to Publix, and maybe we can get some picnic stuff for the trip."

We were planning to drive up to the North Carolina Smokeys the next day. We would get out of Florida's July heat and have some time together as a four-person family. My parents had rented a cabin on the grounds of a Lutheran camp. Our plan was to take a morning course on the book of Daniel and Revelations while Tammy went to childcare.

At the supermarket, Mom picked her up and placed her in the child's seat of a grocery cart. Tammy occupied such a huge place in my mind that I was surprised to see her sitting in the toddler's seat, with room to spare. She was five, but she looked three.

In the produce department, we ran into one of my parents' neighbors.

"Hilda! Guess who this is. My new grandbaby."

Oos, ahs. She was cute.

While Mom fixed supper, Tammy and I went out to the shuffleboard court. She began gathering little pebbles in her Easter pail. I felt grateful that I was not all alone with her this week. I sat on a bench and watched.

For years I felt separated from my parents because of my rejection of their faith. What was central to them had never made any sense to me. Even when I was small and my mother told me to say my prayers, I felt they weren't going anywhere, that I was just saying words in my mind.

Puzzled by my own defection, I wondered if was possible that smart people like my parents and all the other people I knew in the church could all be wrong and all be engaging in a one-way conversation in their heads. Over time, I concluded that this was just what they were doing.

Though belief loomed large in my parents' minds, I saw it as a small thing, a tiny thing in comparison to all it meant to be part of a family. Never did it occur to me that they would be anything but devoted grandparents to any child I brought to them. Tammy would have a family she could trust. My mother would pour herself into guiding her to care about others, to be proud of herself, to know she had family behind her. My father would always light up when he saw her. She would always know she was special.

Tammy brought me some shells as tiny as her own fingernails, each one a perfect Fibonacci sequence, which had once housed a tiny snail.

"Tammy, look how amazing they are! I've sat out here a million times, and yet I never saw them before. You're going to show me lots and lots of new things, aren't you?"

On the trip the next day, my mother and Tammy took the back seat where mom engaged her in a guessing game. "I'm thinking of something in the car. Can you guess?"

Tammy guessed wildly, so Mom tried to teach her what it meant to get warmer or to get colder. Tammy didn't catch on. Frustrated, she began to hit her head with her fist. "Whoa, whoa," said Mom. "It's okay."

But Tammy was lost in misery. I began to sing "John Jacob Jingleheimer Schmitt." Tammy stopped wailing to listen. This song gets progressively softer, but you always belt out the "Tra la la la la" refrain. My father, completely tone deaf, joined in to swell the chorus. When the loud part came, Tammy put her head in her hands, laughing.

"I'm surprised," said Mom. "I never thought that would work."

We spent the night in Valdosta and then sang our way to the cool air of the mountains. Tammy began to get warmer at getting warmer.

As we unloaded the car, Tammy spotted a decorative well in the next yard. My father said, "Let's go see the old oaken bucket." He sang her the song with admirable syncopation on the word BUCK-et , as they walked over to examine the pail. Everything he sang usually sounded like Gregorian chant. In the Lutheran service, he had to chant the greeting, "The Lord be with you," mercifully all on one note. Now, he chuckled as she held his hand, trying to sing along. "The old oaken BUCKet, the ironbound BUCKet." He was once again the playful daddy of my early childhood who would get down on the floor with us and sing, "Fifty men on a boarding house bed. Roll over. Roll over." And he and my brother and I would roll across the floor of our living room.

Tammy went to childcare without an issue, just as she had gone to the June program in New York. After the morning class, I carried her into the camp's big pool where she clung to me as she warily watched the rowdy campers splash and dunk. Suddenly someone called, "Let's rock this pool," and everyone in the water agitated arms and legs until the pool was full of whitecaps. Tammy held tight to me, but I saw that by the end of the week she would be making waves herself.

My mother was from North Carolina, one of twelve brothers and sisters. Most still lived in Kings Mountain, a small town in the Piedmont area about an hour from where we were. My Aunt Ginny drove up for lunch. Tammy was getting into the swing of things and tried to tell Aunt Ginny some of her adventures. Aunt Ginny drawled, "You sure are sweet, Darlin', but I can't understand a word you say."

My cousin Anita came up with her two daughters to meet Tammy and to bring us to Kings Mountain. We were going to spend the night there and then fly home from Charlotte while my parents drove back to Florida.

When we left the cabin, said goodbye to my parents, and got into Anita's car, Tammy became hysterical. She was desperate, inconsolable, screaming for Nana and Poppop.

Anita, a social worker who had supervised many heartbreaking scenes of children torn from homes they loved, said, "Okay, Tammy. You're not ready to go. That's all right." She doubled back and Tammy flew out of the car to my mother.

"Now say 'bye'," said Anita, in her calming North Carolina drawl. "You'll see Nana and Poppop again soon."

I thought of how peacefully she left important people in her life—Bonnie, Foree, Lyle, and Roxana. I wondered if she was having a delayed reaction or if she realized that this was her permanent family.

"That was interesting," said Anita.

Back to New York, I rocked Tammy every night with a medley of lullabies my mother had sung to me. Sometimes Tammy was still wide-awake when I came to the end of my repertoire, so I began verse after verse of Cumbaya. I maxed out at sixteen Cumbayas – someone's teaching the subjunctive to AP French students, Cumbaya. Someone needs to grade papers, Cumbaya. While I sang, I wondered how I would repair all that had been broken in her spirit.

I liked the idea promulgated by the child placement world that adopted children can become grafts on the family tree, but I figured they need proximity for the implant to take. I wanted Tammy to have a sense of belonging that would help her recover from all the times she set down tender roots only to have them torn away. But what did I have to offer her?

The landscape of my childhood, a neighborhood in the west end of Plainfield, New Jersey, remains, but everything that animated it, its soul, has long since evaporated. On summer evenings, we would step out of our homes into the lingering twilight. The grown-ups would chat as the kids pursued fireflies, hoping to catch them with mason jars, air holes in the lids. From kindergarten to eighth grade I walked to Jefferson School. I felt so archetypically American, strolling along with Carol, a Catholic, and Masha, a Jew. We all belonged. But now, Jefferson School was an office building. Plainfield High, scene of my indifferent academic achievement and thespian triumphs, had been torn down, replaced by alien bricks. My father's thriving Lutheran church succumbed, as Germans and Norwegians drifted off into the mid-west, to be replaced by the secular or the charismatic. The hospital where I was born, where my mother left her appendix, and my father, his cecum, folded.

Yet Plainfield stayed as real to me as the Combray that opened up for Proust when he tasted the little madeleine. Would that Tammy would have in her own memory such a permanent sense of place. Could the twelve-month indoor rinks of New York rival the frozen lagoon in Greenbrook Park, at the end of my street, available only when the temperature plummeted? Could the magical city that beckoned to me throughout my childhood retain any of its charm when it was all a child knew? Could its terrain and landmarks at least spell home?

The first year I taught eighth grade, I relived my own eighth grade year. Now with this five-year-old, whose past was almost entirely buried and inaccessible to either one of us, memories of my own childhood flooded in. Toward the end of World War II, my brother and his friends dug foxholes behind the garage. They were about eight or nine, and I was four. I could hear them going "bang bang," shooting with sticks that had been dead wood on the apple tree. I put on my Red Cross armband and went into the pantry to secure supplies for them. I found a big brown bag and put Graham crackers and raisins in it. When they saw me, they stopped shooting for a moment to grab a snack. My brother, deep in the war game, went along with my role. "Thanks, nurse," he said.

My brother was nice to me.

I came running inside, aglow with happiness, and said to my mother, 'I'm going to be a nurse.'

"I thought you wanted to be a missionary," she said.

"A missionary-nurse," I said.

I had found a tiny toehold into what could make me happy.

Tammy had two brothers to play with. Steven and Chris were away in Alabama, but Matthew and Martin lived with Shaunie across town from us. Every other week these two came over to play. Tammy was right between them in age. Matt was 18 months older and Martin was 18 months younger. Usually an au pair came with them, and we would go to the playground and watch them run around on the edge of madness. Once in the summer when Stuyvesant Town had turned on the big showers in the playgrounds, the two boys ran smack into each other under the tumbling water. They both had goose eggs. I said to the au pair, "No wonder the parents gave them up – no one could manage five like this."

I asked adult Tammy what she remembered about the playgrounds of Stuyvesant Town.

> —I remember one day it was me, Matthew, and Martin on a playground and Martin was being such a jerk, and Matt pushed him off the jungle gym and he got mad and he pushed Matt on the ground after that and I remember I tagged both of them and said, "You're it." And I ran up towards the jungle gym and started climbing. And they said, "Hey, wait a second," and they started climbing. And that sort of broke the push kinda shove kinda thing.
> —So you were a kind of peace maker.
> —Well, they didn't kill each other.

Despite their long separation in various foster homes, or perhaps because of this, the five children felt attached to each other. Tammy and Matt, particularly, had a powerful bond. Poor Martin was often left in the dust with his stuffed animals. Matt sought Tammy's approval and shared with her his passion for He-Man, Master of the Universe. Tammy became the esteemed ally of He-Man/Matt in the persona of She-Ra, He-Man's incredibly strong twin. With his Sword of Power and her Sword of Protection they repeatedly managed to vanquish the evil Skeletor, whom Matt loathed with righteous fervor.

While Matt worshiped his sister, my own brother had wanted me to disappear. For the past sixty-five years, he has been a true, kind, devoted brother,
so it seems a little unfair to bring up the 1940's. What can you do? Our childhood was what it was, and in 1940, when I was born, he was a three-and-a-
half-year-old king, about to have to share the throne with a dumb baby. He
didn't like it. I was Abel to his Cain, though unlike Adam and Eve apparently,
our parents had strict rules about killing your sibling. No sticks and stones.

Words were another matter. He made up songs and names. He sang,
"Margie the ignorant, googoogoo." He called me "Faceless." "Your face is not
so bad—you just don't happen to have one." I looked in the mirror; I did have
a face. "Faceless" soon evolved to "Less" and then to "Lester."

When I, with bitter tears, complained to my mother that Joey was mean
to me she said, "Brothers are like that. I had three older brothers. You have to
give it back."

Giving it back was not in my skill set, but I took to heart the notion that
this was just how brothers are. In truth, I loved my brother. I was the embodi-
ment of Carmen's aria about the food chain of love: *Si tu ne m'aimes pas je
t'aime – mais si tu m'aimes prends garde à toi.* (If you don't love me, I love you
—but if you love me, watch out for yourself). I was his virtual lawyer when
Mom came after him for neglecting some duty. But the person who needed
to watch out for me was my father. As dismissive as my brother was to me,
my father was sweet and loving. He lived the dictum "Turn the other cheek."
I took out every verbal blow from my brother on my father, who responded
always with passive kindness. There was no limit to the amount of sassy im-
patience he would take from me. "My glasses are dirty," I would exclaim petu-
lantly as I left for school, as though this were somebody's fault.

"Let me clean them," he would say, pleased to be of use to me.

My other response to my brother's teasing was the one that led to seeking
out and finding Tammy: stepped up empathy for the underdog. My mother
suggested that I put myself in the other person's shoes. I became a bleeding

heart. I befriended the outcast girl who came to school dirty and neglected. Nobody would talk to Betty Bruno*. People said she was white trash and that her mother worked at night and that it wasn't nice work. Betty's hard life led her to a love of animals. She had found a litter of stray kittens and wanted to give me one. My mother hated cats, but yielded to my unending pleas to take one of Betty Bruno's kittens.

Eunice, one of the smart girls in the class, asked me, "Why are you talking to Betty Bruno?"

I had no answer. I liked her. Her clothes were dirty and so was her face, but she loved kittens and gave me one. I believed that you should love everyone. That's what I learned in Sunday School, and I believed it.

I raided the pantry to feed the hungry. I put together boxes with pencils and soap for poor people overseas. One day my mother said, "You know what I said about putting yourself in the other person's shoes? Well I take it back. Look out for yourself."

This advice came too late.

I started out showering my dolls with such tender care that they always reeked of Johnsons Baby Powder. I raided the linen closet for towels to swaddle them in and washcloths to clean their rubbery skin. Sally was a diaper doll; I fed her water from tiny bottles and then had to change her. She couldn't drink milk; I tried it once, but the smell coming from inside her was rank. The air cleared up after a long force-feeding of H_2O. Susan was a magic skin doll. Her inability to imbibe did not give her a free pass on powder. I loved them; I sang to them.

From dolls, I escalated to the toddler next door. I read little Janet Sue the story of *Pony Dapple Gray* over and over to merry shrieks. Her mother welcomed me; while she did her chores, I entertained Janet Sue. By the time I was in the seventh grade I had a gaggle of first graders who stopped by every morning on the way to school to hear me read stories like the Chinese Sandman or Shingabiss, Wild Duck of the North.

How different Tammy's play with dolls was. Like the wax choristers at my parents' place, her dolls were lined up in a row for Tammy to instruct. There sat Bear, Panda, Baby (a Cabbage Patch Kid) and Girl on the couch. In strict tones she said, "Panda, woo sit by Bear, not by Baby." She sighed. "Okay, I show you. Panda, woo vewy vewy bad."

—Tammy, remember your dolls?

—No.

—What?

—No. I don't.

—Not Girl? She was your alter ego.

—Sorry.

—What about Panda and Baby.

—Mom, I don't remember them.

No memory of her desperate grief when she left Girl on the Trenton Local? No recollection of pleading with me to call New Jersey Transit over and over as she stomped about and wailed in the background?

For at least a week she carried on with her noisy lamentations until I found another rag doll with the same sewn-on bonnet and the same stern printed face. She greeted Girl II with a euphoria befitting a resurrection.

All this had been deleted from adult Tammy's hard drive. She was like Eve or Sybil after the personality integration.

My parents came to visit me that first fall. "Mom," I said. "I really want Tammy to have roots somewhere. New York is kind of a place for the rootless. What do you think?"

"How much money do you have?" she said.

"About $4000."

"Hmm. I think we could put together a down payment."

So it was settled. With my parents' help, I bought a little house in Kings Mountain, North Carolina, where Tammy could absorb the warmth of small town life, Mom could have some time with her eight remaining siblings, and I could reconnect with the summers of my childhood, when my cousins and I lazed through the days, enjoying watermelon feasts, hand-churned freezers of ice cream, and fish fries in the backyards of my numerous aunts and uncles. What Plainfield was for me during the school year, Kings Mountain was during my summers. But unlike Plainfield, Kings Mountain offered me a present sense of belonging because my cousins had returned there after college, married, settled down, and had their children there.

Tammy and I could escape from our sweltering apartment to our air-conditioned home as soon as school let out. For four summers, my parents, Tammy, and I came to stay and link up with the McGinnises. My mother, whose name was Geraldine but who had always been called Jelly, was the only one of the twelve to have settled outside the Carolinas. They all loved to say, "That Jelly went and ran off with a jack leg Yankee preacher."

—Tammy, what do you remember about Nana?

—She was a nice old lady. She would do needlepoint sometimes. I would sit with her, and she would have a round circling thing with a cloth in it.

—That was quilting.

—No, she had like a circle.

—An embroidery hoop.

—Yeah. And she'd go in and out. She would do like a small little designy in the center. I remember I'd be sitting on the carpety floor and she'd be sitting in the chair and I'd be sitting playing around with things. And she'd just be sitting doing her needle thingy.

As soon as we moved into our little house, my cousin Anita's teenage daughters, Anne and Emily, took Tammy under their wing and picked her up every day to go to vacation church school. Once when young Anne brought her back, she said, "Margie, what's wrong with her? She doesn't stop whining and fussing even when she gets her own way."

"Tell me about it. If I understood, I'd tell you. I know it can drive you nuts."

The tantrums, the sullen silences, the stalking off into the street, the unintelligible speech, the head banging, peeing and pooping in her pants at random times every day – I was going to fix this. If I no longer believed in God, I did believe in the power of love and patience. Either I was right or it was a *folie à deux*.

My mother thought religion was the cure. At dinner, my father would say grace, and Tammy would sneak peeks to see what everyone else was doing. Once when she said, "Oh, God!" my mother told her not to take the name of the Lord in vain. Tammy looked at me perplexed; she had heard me say "Oh God" a hundred times. "Well, I guess God is very busy," I said, "and when you say his name, He has to stop whatever He's doing and it's not right to distract Him from all the stuff in the universe."

"I didn't know you had it in you," my mother said.

"Don't take the law in vain," said Tammy.

When we were little, my cousins and I thought that Uncle Donald was better looking than Gregory Peck. We broke a chair trying to pile onto his lap. He had a factory outside of town where he manufactured a white brick he had invented. A byproduct, which he sold to a pharmaceutical company, was lithium, used in treating bipolar disorder. Many years later, Tammy took this drug to try to control her mood swings. Uncle Donald finally sold the business, but instead of retiring, he bought a farm. Tammy loved it when he came by with armloads of corn. "There's nothing like this silver queen," he said. It was the sweetest, most tender, smallest kernelled white corn imaginable. Nothing in the supermarkets compared. As I sat in our carport and shucked it, Tammy collected the little worms lodged in the silk and talked to them as though they were wax choristers.

Every afternoon we went out to Lake Montonia, where we had had a cabin when I was Tammy's age. My mother sat in a rocker, chatting with the old timers while Tammy and I went in the water. We both squealed wading in because a big fish nipped at us if we got too near the nest of eggs she was protecting. Tammy learned to swim in the very lake where so many years before I had first taken my feet off the bottom doing the dead man's float.

Tammy and I were by ourselves. There were other people there, but we didn't know them. None of the young cousins frequented the lake. Times had changed. People had pools in their backyards. When I was a child any-one could go to the lake, use the dressing rooms, and buy Moon Pies and Butterfingers at the concession stand.

The stand was gone, and now the lake was a gated community. You had to pay to belong. Membership was limited to those living around the lake and their families. Luckily for us, my Uncle Bill had a house there.

Fun places like lakes and cocktail parties can be the loneliest places on earth. Everyone is joking and gossiping, but there you are, standing or swim-ming, outside and alone.

Nostalgic as I was for the days when all the splashing kids around me were my cousins, I was still happy to have this time with my mother. It turned out that these summers were for Mom more than for us. This town was her home. Tammy had the experience of a powerful, laughing grandmother, who was of course the source of my ridiculous, against all odds, maternal drive. She made motherhood look essential.

EDUCATION

Setting down roots and being loved were only the first strands to be pulled from of the tangled skein of Tammy's needs. She came to me already formed, with a prior life and prior memories. And those memories called up terrifying insecurity. Biological children have no reason to question that they are in the right place. Even children adopted as babies feel a trust unknown to older adoptees, whose early childhood consisted of a series of disruptions. Foster children, at the bottom of the totem pole, have no reason to believe that their serial placements will ever end. Though I couldn't give Tammy the security of adoption, I could tell her what I believed. Back in New York, as we walked by the splashing waters of the fountain in Stuyvesant Town's grassy oval on the way to school, she said, "I wanna stay with you."

"Don't worry Tammy. You're staying with me. If Bonnie ever comes back, what do you think I'll do?"

She looked perplexed.

I bent down and looked her in the eye. "I'll punch her in the nose." Tammy laughed her head off.

Though overwhelmed, at least I had the school. I could offer her Jane and Judy's most wonderful of all kindergartens at Friends Seminary, a much-coveted entry-level placement for the five-year-olds of NYC. I imagined the Mommy and Me crowd sitting on the benches of New York's playgrounds discussing how to pad the admissions packet to maximize their little one's chances of being dusted with the Jane and Judy magic. I loved the spacious room, alive with bright primary colors and inviting stations, where the children could develop small motor and big mental skills.

Tammy could not help but be different from the rest in this setting, but I hoped she would learn from her peers. Very early she showed that she had not acquired some of the basic lessons the others got in preschool. Jane told me that every time she got the group ready to go outside to the playground, Tammy would disappear into the cubbies where the kids kept their coats. Jane was determined to change this behavior. She made a chart and Tammy got a star every time she went out to the playground appropriately. After five stars, I would reward her with a coloring book. Tammy began to get coloring books regularly. She made friends with a little girl names Alicia. I saw progress.

—Tammy, what do you remember about Friends Seminary?

—I remember Steve Pratt, tall, medium build, gym teacher. I remember him. He was nice and fun to hang out with and I remember when I was on that boat ride that he understood about me being sick.

—Do you remember Jane and Judy?

—I remember Jill. I think that was the one that I remember – tall dark hair.

—Jill was Paul's teacher. It was Jane and Judy.

 – Oh. Not sure. It was either Jane or Judy – she had dark hair like black she was tall, slender. She was very patient. I remember that she was very patient with me because I remember I had a lot of trouble with certain things and she would just sometimes she would just sit next to me try to help me step by step "This is how   you   do this." You know. "This is how you do that." That's all I remember. She was very patient I remember looking at her being very patient; she would just sit down next to me and try to help me with what-ever I'm struggling with. She's just sitting there all nice and patient. I remember looking at her and thinking how can the person be so patient, I'm going nuts; it's frustrating for me. She's just sitting there just nice and patient. I couldn't figure it out.

—What about Kathy

—Kathy—she had kind of 1960's hair big poof; she reminded me of like a reporter in the 1960's with big poufy hair and stuff. She had a lot of patience too.

SPECIAL SEVICES

On the education front I really got it right. But after all my big talk to the world and to myself that Tammy's placement with me was her ticket to all the services she needed, I had to face the reality that I had no idea where to look.

One day, as we were walking along, she saw a picture of Superman. "Tuperman!" she said. Oh my God, she could say the "t" sound. She just had some crossed consonant wires.

"Tammy," I said, "say Sammy."

"Tammy," she said.

She said it perfectly. Where was my lantern? I wanted to run through the streets shouting, Eureka. "That's it! That's your name. Say it again."

"Tammy."

"YES!" And she never said it wrong again.

"Tammy. Tammy. Tammy."

"By George, you've got it!"

So by trial and error, she made progress.

Still, it was a drop in the bucket. In these pre-Google days, I turned to the yellow pages, where I looked up "speech." There I found one listing for speech therapy and it happened to be a few blocks away at an institution called the International Center for the Disabled. I called up and was immediately assigned a speech therapist named Julie.

Julie did an assessment and discovered that in addition to the very apparent articulation issues, Tammy was missing several parts of speech. She had no possessive adjectives, for instance, and used pronouns instead –"me cat," "you school."

Tammy looked forward to her weekly sessions with Julie, who, among many other activities, had Tammy look at pictures of multisyllabic items like binoculars and alligators, and then encouraged her to say all four syllables. Within a year, Tammy had all the parts of speech and would no longer strike people as speech impaired. Julie said that she probably would always have some pronunciation issues, but she was officially finished with speech therapy. I considered this Tammy's first and most thrilling success in the world of support services.

Therapy to deal with her emotions was another matter. Someone told me about the Post Graduate Center. After an assessment, they informed me she needed two sessions per week and that I needed one.

"Me! What do I need therapy for?"

"This will benefit her."

Once, years earlier, I went to a fortuneteller on Third Avenue with my friend Karen and a travel buddy of hers named Tina. The psychic took one look at Karen and said, "You no like nobody give you no trouble."

To me she said, "You no like give nobody no trouble." I thought she might be the real deal when she looked at Tina's palm and said, "You have two children."

"No," said Tina triumphantly. "I have three."

The gypsy took a closer look at her hand. "Funny, I only see two pregnancies."

A frisson passed through the little group when Tina said, "Well, I have twins."

She got me right too. My body language must have said it all. I felt helpless as I saw my life fill up with appointments. One afternoon a week I already had a faculty meeting, and another, Tammy had speech. Now I had to take her to therapy one more afternoon, and then Saturday mornings we would do back to back sessions., one for me and one for her. When was she supposed to play? When were we supposed to live our lives? When would we have time to have dinner with Hal followed by the treat of Tammy dancing? So often in those pre-therapy days, she would put on her cassette of Rainbow Bright, and as she had in the mall, pour her soul into dance, her face focused and stern. Dance, she needed time to dance.

—Tammy, what do music and dance mean to you?

—Well they both are a way to express and be creative. It's the way I express myself. I'm a very creative person. Plus it's one of the strong things that I have.

—Is dance the most important thing in your life?

—No. My kid is the most important thing. But I would rate it maybe like an eight. First it's my kid, then my dog, then dance and music and art.

—What kind of dance do you do?

—I do all – I do reggae, Spanish, hip hop, country, contemporary. All of it.

A MOM

With all these appointments, by the time we got home, we barely had time for her to eat, bathe, and, spend time with her homework books. I would have to get a baby sitter for her when I went in for my session. I consulted with one of my most mature high school students, and she suggested a swap– her sister needed a little help with French grammar at the Spence School. While Tammy was in her session, I tutored the sister in the cramped waiting room. In return, my Friends student came and watched Tammy when I went in.

While I was in my session, I could hear Tammy tearing around out of control while my student did her best to corral her. I told the therapist that it didn't seem to make sense for me to chat with her when Tammy needed me, and I didn't need therapy.

"This is for Tammy," she said

"If it's for her, how come her Medicaid isn't paying for it?"

It seemed to me that this was just a one-size-fits-all policy. All the parents of troubled children who walked through the door had to meet with the therapist. Maybe some other parents had caused the problem. Or maybe they didn't have a range of strategies. My case was different, or so I thought. I spent most of my life with kids. And I could hardly be blamed for Tammy's issues. I couldn't very well have screwed her up from afar.

It took me a year, but I finally figured out that Saturdays had to be free. Too bad I didn't have time for assertiveness training. I needed it. But when I thought that taking charge was for Tammy, I could do it. I told The Post Graduate Center that I wanted Tammy to come once a week. Period. They felt I was wrong, but I knew that Tammy and I needed more time to become mother and daughter. In the end, they yielded, but since the therapist was going on maternity leave, I seized the opportunity to make a break. We went to St. Vincent's where her brothers, Matthew and Martin, were in treatment. There, one session per week was the norm.

The first of my newly freed-up Saturdays, I climbed up into the top level of her loft, big enough for her to stand, but I had to sit on the carpet we'd put up there. All those coloring books came in handy, and we talked about animals as we colored. She had extended her spectrum from black first to purple and black and now finally to the whole panoply of the 48-crayon box.

As we colored, I asked how school was going.

"Good."

"Yes? What are you learning?

"George Washington was the president."

"Wow. Is he still the president?"

"No, now it's Ronald McDonald."

So cute, it was tempting not to correct her.

We opened the toy chest and found little figures and buildings to make a neighborhood with smiling merchants and police officers. The idea, I guess, was that a friendly merchant and police officer might make the reality out there seem more welcoming.

In the afternoon, we went to see Goonies at the movies. Walking back from Kips Bay on First Avenue, we passed the donut shop we frequented after speech therapy. Tammy began whining about vanilla frosting and rainbow sprinkles. I said, "Why don't we wait and get a Popsicle from Larry. " When we turned onto Twentieth Street, the artery between Stuyvesant Town and Peter Cooper Village, we spotted Larry with his cart and parasol at the corner of Twentieth and the North Loop. Tammy went running.

"Tammy, how's my girl?" he called.

"I saw Goonies. There was a boat. Can I have a Popsicle?"

"How's it going, Larry?" I said.

"Great! Some of my works are being shown at a gallery in SoHo!" Our ice cream man was as friendly as the miniatures in Tammy's loft. Like many New Yorkers, he used his day job to support his artistic passion. He gave me a postcard with a picture of one of his abstracts.

"That's fantastic. We'll try to go."

We headed on toward home, passing the door to Hal's building right next to our one deli. By the time we got to D'Agostino's Supermarket, we could see the river and the FDR Drive.

"I think Girl is in trouble," she said.

"Girl's in trouble?" Girl, the rag doll with the last name Allereego, was a known rapscallion. Tammy chided her every day.

"Uh-huh. Maybe she's in trouble because she went down to the river."

"The river?"

"Uh-huh. With a bad guy. Maybe she's in trouble."

"Well, did she know he was a bad guy?"

"No! She thought he was a good guy when she went."

"Well then, Tammy, it's not Girl's fault, is it? She didn't go with a bad guy on purpose."

Tammy gave this some thought. "Okay."

What had she told me? Some long-buried bogeyman—a caretaker? a stranger? an older child?—had bubbled up out of her unconscious. I was her sixth home. What was the likelihood that nothing abusive had happened in all those places? Girl went down to the river with a bad guy. Something bad happened; the details were lost forever. Guilt and fear lingered.

"You know Mommy loves you."

"I know," she said, in that bored, annoyed tone that said, "Not that again."

It was inadequate. I agree.

So much was hidden. I clung to the hope that St. Vincent's would cure her.

FACE IT: A LITTLE GIRL IS NOT A LUMP OF CLAY

The first therapist at St. Vincent's, a very kind and cheerful Sri Lankan, broke her foot in an exercise class and was out of commission for several months. No sooner did she begin again with Tammy than she left. The new therapist was an intern and also destined to leave.

With hesitation (as I 'no like give nobody no trouble'), I spoke with the director. I felt ill making waves, but I knew that standing up for Tammy was my unquestionable duty. "Look, you're telling me that separation is her big issue, and she gets a new therapist every eight months or so. Shouldn't she have one person all the way through until high school?"

They gave her a staff person who indeed was with her until she got married. Why hadn't I put my foot down when she was five? Now she was eight. It was one thing for me to put up with all manner of inconvenience and discomfort because I was too mealy mouthed to speak up. But now I had to be Tammy's voice in the world. I felt with urgency that I had to change, release my inner bitch. I knew she was in there somewhere. My family certainly knew it.

This therapist was a social worker named Gerry Natwin, and I immediately felt she was both empathetic and practical. Soon into her sessions with Tammy she told me that Tammy had PDD-NOS,—Pervasive Developmental Disorder Not Otherwise Specified. I had never heard of it. When I looked it up, I found that it was an autism spectrum condition.

The *Diagnostic and Statistical Manual of Mental Disorders* put out by the American Psychiatric Association seems to redefine it every few years, but generally PDD-NOS, I discovered, is characterized more by what it is not than what it is. It's not autism, where three distinct areas are affected: social interaction, verbal communication, and repetitive movement. It's not Asperger's (which comes and goes in the DSM) where verbal development is pretty much normal, but where social interaction and repetitive behaviors might be involved. Asperger's kids, unlike those with Autism, have good vocabularies and can speak informatively. They are usually smart. Some, like Sherlock Holmes and House, (not real people, but based on Asperger's types) figure out over time how to cope very effectively.

Pervasive Developmental Disorder – Not Otherwise Specified is not so well defined. It turns out to be a large bin in which to stash odd kids, kids who have their own peculiar combination of social issues, verbal issues and repetitive behaviors. They might have a dramatic impairment in one area but very little unusual in the other two. A child who flails his arms, talks a little funny, but still communicates and makes friends might have PDD.

Sometimes people didn't notice right away that there was anything odd about Tammy. When she was relaxed, she smiled and charmed and seemed fine. As the first psychologist told me when I had her tested at age five, it didn't hurt that she was attractive. She never had an issue with eye contact.

If she was worried or stressed, she might seem tactless or bizarre. She once asked someone getting on an elevator with us, "What's your name?" When the lady answered, "Gwen," she said, "That's an ugly name." For ten floors, I had to wonder if there was anything I could say that would not make the situation worse. Another time a man got on and pressed the button for the eleventh floor. I tightened up, hoping there would be no repetition of the "Gwen Incident."

"What's your name?" she asked.

He got down on her level, looked her in the eye, and said, "Gwen."

It turned out he was Gwen's husband, and for once, Tammy was stopped in her tracks.

She would stray behind me as we walked home from school, attract the attention of a stranger, and then mention that mommy was leaving her. One woman threatened to call the authorities to report my neglect of the poor child. Here's what I wanted to say: Keep your opinions to yourself or take a little walk in my moccasins, bitch.

My thoughts (clearly) can be every bit as indelicate as Tammy's, but here's the difference between her and me: I don't say them out loud.

Her dramatic mood swings contribute to social impairment. When she was up, she talked endlessly and repetitively. I marveled at her ability to re-plow the same terrain. Just when you thought a full stop was imminent, there was more.

"Amy has a new kitty and it is sweet not like Mushy Mushy, a nice sweet kitty you can pet and I petted it. Amy's kitty is sweet and lets you pet her. Not like Mushy Mushy. I mean, Mushy won't let people pet her, but Amy's kitty will. You know what I mean? ". . . .So, yes, she was and is socially impaired.

She came to me with an obvious verbal deficiency. When the speech therapist indicated that the goals of therapy had been met, she also mentioned that Tammy would probably always have trouble with big words and would generally demonstrate a small level of impairment. Often I tried to help her.

"I pacifically told him."

"No Tammy, not pacifically, specifically."

"Whatever. I did tell him."

(She still says "pacifically.")

Often I didn't interrupt her thought.

"Paparazzi is such a great tenor," or "Moonlight Sinatra is so beautiful."

She loved to watch figure skating. "Did you hear? Kristie fell. She might have a fraction." "Michele won because she was the only one who could do a triple klutz."

In the rain, she got drenched as a bone. When she left her contact lens in too long, her eye was pitch red. The heroine was rescued in the nick of a dime. We should take care of things right away. "Nip it in the butt."

In school, she loved rely races, which seems to me a more expressive term than the real one. Her headaches were always mindgrains.

Apart from these malapropisms, which do happen every day, she is able to express herself with a high degree of clarity. She is, after all, my daughter, and I love to gab with her. She can go on a tear about wrestling or NASCAR races. She knows the ins and outs, marriages and divorces and a few more sordid details of the major players. When we talk about TV shows or movies, I love her read on the characters. "Let me tell you girlfriend," she'll say to me. When a character does something stupid she'll exclaim, "Oh no she did-in'!" And then do a perfect Valley Girl shrug of disgust. When I ask her to do something she is not about to do she says, "That's not a no, that's a hell no."

As to repetitive behaviors, when she was little, she did bang her head with her hand and when she was anxious she would rock. After she was six or so, PDD experts would be hard pressed to find much here.

So she was tossed into this bin, but I'm not sure if she had much in common with the other kids in there with her. Tammy made eye contact, and she was sociable though odd.

The symptoms I noticed were that she wet her pants and pooped in them during the day with a fair degree of regularity up until the fifth grade. That's enuresis and encopresis. She also sometimes went crazy and acted like a toddler. That's regression. She fussed and fumed, resisted any suggestions, refused food and stomped about in a cloud of negativity. I think that's oppositional personality. These last two symptoms never really went away.

I did not find enuresis, encopresis, regression, and oppositional personality when I read about PDD-NOS.

I also did not find a trait which has persisted to this day: she maintained a casual adherence to the truth. One day at Friends, Jane came up to me looking very concerned. "Marge, how are you?"

"Fine."

"Tammy told me about the accident."

Amazing. We hadn't even been in a car.

I guess those are all signs of something. But there seemed to me to be vagueness in the diagnosis. Oh well. If they wanted to give her a diagnosis, that was fine with me.

It seems there was a slight discrepancy between my idea of therapy and the reality of therapy. I just wanted to fix her. I thought Tammy would slough her symptoms the way a snake sheds its skin. The world of therapy thought I had better get used to what I had.

—What about Miss Natwin?

—We just played and talked. That's all I remember about.

—Miss Natwin was your therapist from when you were eight until you got married. Do you think she helped you?

—I don't know.

4

LIVING LIFE

We spent our summers with my mother's side of the family in Kings Mountain, but for our Christmas and spring breaks, Tammy and I headed to Fort Myers, Florida to visit my parents. My paternal grandfather grew up in this town, one of the eight children of Manuel A and Evalina Weatherford Gonzalez, the first settlers. A sea captain from Asturias, Spain, Manuel, my great grandfather, had the task of bringing the mail from Key West, where he was living, to the soldiers in the old fort, already called Fort Myers. In February of 1866, he sailed up the Caloosahatchee with his little son Manny and found the fort deserted. Within a few weeks, his wife arrived to join them. According to local lore, the Gonzalez family lived for a time in the abandoned fort.

My grandfather was born in Fort Myers. In his early years, his mother, Evalina, the town's first teacher, educated him. She began with her own kids, and then as the population grew, she welcomed the children of new settlers. My grandfather developed an interest in journalism, and ended up as a printer in New York.

When my parents retired, they began to spend winters in Fort Myers reestablishing connections with cousins. My father was seventy when they decided to buy a condo of their own. Seventy seemed like an advanced age to me at the time, but it turned out that my father had more than two decades left to enjoy the semi-tropics.

Tammy and I particularly loved visiting my father's cousin, Charlton Tooke, son of my grandfather's sister Lavinia. He had a sprawling grove along highway 41 in North Fort Myers, across from the touristy Shell Factory. The first time I visited him, before I had Tammy, his wife Irene was still alive. An avid reader, she had lost her sight and spent her time listening to audio-books while Charlton tended the trees. He was one of those Florida crackers who got their name from the way they cracked their whips when they were rounding up cattle. Now in his 80's, he sat down with us and reminisced about the long-ago days when he was a cowboy "out ta Punta Rassa." He said he never left Florida in his life. "No, no, no – don't want to go up in that cold. Never did see snow in my whole life, though."

"So Charlton," I said, "how long have you been tending this grove?"

"Put in the trees when I was sixty-five."

I was stunned. I thought he would say that he had been raising citrus fruit for much of his adult life. You can begin something at sixty-five and see it come to fruition. My view that the curve of life's achievements nose-dived at sixty-five was upended.

Attached to his house by a breezeway was another smaller house where Charlton's son, Joe Tooke, lived. He administered a social service agency in town and was warmly valued for his skill and empathy.

When I brought Tammy out for the first time, Joe took us into his place to see his sulfur crested cockatoo. Tammy, still somewhat unintelligible, began to converse with the bird, who apparently had no difficulty understanding her. The cockatoo was his prize, but out in the yard he had built a long lovely habitat, which would have been the pride of any zoo, for his collection of smaller exotic birds. Tammy and I looked with awe at the twittery finches in various shades of blue, green, and yellow. Adjacent to the birds, were green-houses. Joe showed us his collection of orchids, some of which he sometimes entered in competitions.

"Okay," he said. "Let's get some bags and pick some oranges. What do you say, Tammy?" Out she ran, pulling down low hanging tangelos, so ripe that they were pure juice wrapped in a container of peel. It seemed possible to stick a straw in one and drink the juice straight out.

Joe and I got to talking and lost sight of Tammy momentarily. "Where is she? We have to find her fast – there are fire ants out there. Ah, there you are. You better stay with us, Sweetie. There are ants out there that bite. You don't want to meet up with them." We went back to my parents' laden with fruit.

Even more important than Florida's wondrous fruit, birds and orchids was my parents' cozy condo. Tammy took a tangelo, sat down in front of the TV, and put the videotape of *Amadeus* in the slot. *Amadeus* was all she wanted to see. If I had to guess, I would say she watched it through at least 50 times. When I asked her if she thought that 50 was about right, she said, "More like 100." Once when we were riding in the car, I had the classical music station on. I recognized the piece as Mozart but I didn't know what it was.

"Tammy was this piece in the movie?"

She was incredulous. "You don't remember?"

"No, do you?"

"That's where the oboe takes it away from the clarinet," she said.

One morning, back in New York, Tammy was already playing with her dolls when I got up. I went to put in my contacts and discovered that the case was open and the lenses were missing. Where could they be? This was going to be a bad day. I wouldn't be able to see.

"Tammy, do you know where my contacts are? They were in this little case."

"No."

Uh-oh. There was a look of guilt. I had to be careful not to push her into a corner if I ever wanted my contacts back.

"It's okay, Tammy. I just need them to see."

"Dunno."

I was afraid they were already down the drain or flushed away. Putting myself in her mind, I thought *aha cute little cases. I must know what is inside. Nothing important. I shall dump them.* Creeping around the floor of the bathroom, I suddenly noticed the slight glint among the very foul grains of kitty litter. Kitty litter again!

"Tammy my contact lenses are in the disgusting kitty litter and if I ever wear them again I'll probably go blind. I can't believe you did this! Enough with the kitty litter! It's where Mushy Mushy goes to the bathroom for pity sake. No floating water in it. No putting anything in it."

My voice was rising into its highest register as I vented my rage. I was off the floor and now towering over her. "I can't believe it! I can't believe you would do this." Up and up went my voice.

Tammy came back at me with a hitherto unheard coloratura. "Ahahah AH AH AH AH AH ah ah ah," she sang in glorious arpeggio, her voice soaring into territory where glasses break.

It was the Queen of the Night from the Magic Flute. Dozens of times Tammy and I had seen Mozart compose this aria in his head as his mother-in-law yelled at him. *Where's Constanze,"* he would ask.

I told her! I told her myself. Go to a spa! Get your health back! That's what I told her!

Mozart transformed the bitchy woman's complaint into art. Tammy once again outfoxed me. She transformed my wrath into comedy.

Friends Seminary had a policy that no one could have a birthday party without inviting the whole class, or rather you could have a small party, but not one where the whole class was invited except for one or two. As a result, Tammy had an enviable social life. Once when I asked Tammy if she would like to go to the movies, she said, "Let's go to a birthday party."

When she was in the second grade, a family in Elizabeth, NJ, invited her to an ice skating rink for their son's party. We took the short ride on the Trenton local and made our way to the rink. Tammy had never heard of skating before. Michelle and Nat, the parents of young Michael, welcomed us warmly. A table was laden with chips, veggies, dips, and drinks. When everyone had arrived, the kids put on skates and went out on the ice. Most held the side wall as their feet slid out from under them. Some hit the ice hard, but bounced right back up.

As soon as Tammy's skates were laced, she headed purposefully to the rink and went straight out. After making a few strides to build up speed she glided all the way around the large oval.

A father standing next to me watched his daughter cling to the side. When confident Tammy sailed by as though she had been on skates her whole life, he said, "Where does Tammy take lessons?"

"Actually, this is the first time she has even seen ice. I must have forgotten to tell her to be careful."

Michelle came over to watch too. We saw Tammy catch up with Michael and imitate him bending forward with his hands clasped behind his back.

"You have a skater," said Michelle.

"So do you."

"Yes, but Michael has been coming to this rink every week for the past two years."

As we were leaving, Michelle said, "Maybe you and Tammy would like to come out again next weekend to skate. Or—I have an idea –has Tammy ever been skiing?"

"Well, no. And neither have I for that matter. "

"Well, there's supposed to be snow at Craigsmeer. Come out and I'll drive you to what passes for a mountain in the Garden State. Maybe she'll take to the slopes."

Though I grew up in New Jersey, I never knew you could ski there.

"You can spend the night. We're going to a concert in Plainfield on Saturday, so come along."

Michelle didn't know us at all, so this was a generous gesture, and I knew I should be grateful. But I had never felt the remotest interest in skiing. I figured it would be like the dreadful out of control feeling you got on a roller coaster. Then again, Tammy loved roller coasters. So I said, "Sure, we'd love to."

Saturday morning, on the train to Elizabeth, I watched Tammy pull a gaggle of Barbies out of her bag and line then up to give them instruction. The shapely adults had displaced Girl, Panda and Bear.

So this is what being a parent was. Instead of drawing her into my world of school and books, I would be the tagalong. Watching her in the playgrounds of Stuyvesant Town and Central Park, waiting for her at the bottom of Alpine slides in summer, figuring out what to do with all the horseshoe crabs she brought back from the beach, sitting while she looped the loop at Great Adventure, this is what it was. So we would go skiing. All my thought had been of how I would open doors for Tammy. Turns out she was opening them for me.

Tammy did indeed take to the slopes. As soon as she got her skis on, Michael took her with him to the easiest slope. A lesson was included in the price, so I decided to take one. There was a minuscule hill outside the lodge. The instructor told me to "snowplow" (a technique unknown to me) and then to fall.

"Fall," he said over and over.

I was heading straight toward him. If in that millisecond I could form a thought, it was, "Fall? Are you kidding me? All my life I have been instructed not to fall. I don't want to fall."

I fell. Right on top of the instructor. Tammy was out there enjoying life without a lesson, and I was picking myself up out of the snow, apologizing profusely.

I returned the skis and found Michelle. She said that it had never occurred to her to do anything but *après-ski*. It turned out that Michael was adopted too, although as an infant. We both had children who would surprise us with talents we ourselves didn't possess.

Of course all children present surprises because of nature's way of shuffling and sifting the genes, but adopted children, like friends, like spouses, regale us with new and unexpected vistas. "Ski slope" which had previously been a cold, insignificant term was now animated by the little figure of Tammy, thrilling to the swift downhill slide. Every so often I caught sight of her jumping off the ski lift. Immediately, she disappeared down the mountain.

That evening the ski party settle in pews for a concert at the Crescent Avenue Presbyterian Church, just a few blocks from my alma mater, Plainfield High. I thought Tammy would be tired from skiing and would perhaps fall asleep, but she was not about to settle. She fussed and squirmed until I had to take her out. We walked around on the street, so familiar to me from my high school days. She cried and whined.

"It's okay, Tammy. We don't have to go to the concert. "

She kept up the fuss.

"Well, what is it. What's the matter?"

"I'll tell you why," she said with a foot stomp. "I hate my mother!"

By now, I was her mother.

"What color is your mother's hair?"

"Yellow!" she sobbed.

Yellow was Bonnie. Not me. Well, I was glad it wasn't me, but sad that Bonnie could still be referred to as her mother.

When everyone went back to Michelle and Nat's, I was chatting with another mother from Friends. I told her what Tammy had said. "She said she hated her mother – not me, by the way."

"I'm impressed," she said. "It took me fifteen years of therapy to spit that one out."

Early on, like everyone, I discovered the two great new realities of parenthood – the ubiquity of the child and laundry, which she produced in abundance. At first, I couldn't leave Tammy alone at all. Every time I took clothes to the laundry room in the basement of the building, she had to come along. The day she said she would rather not come downstairs with me – she would prefer to stay and play—was a milestone. Eventually I was able to run to the store and leave her in the apartment. But for those early years, I had a constant companion. We went everywhere together.

And we had settled in. Tammy had new friends. She skied, skated, biked, hiked, and danced. Old friends visited, too, like Sroeun, who came by from time to time. She told me that she had a new little brother; her mother had a baby. So that was the stock Sroeun came from. Her mother's children had been stolen from her and killed, but from some inner reach she was able to choose to continue to live.

Sroeun took Tammy out to the playground and climbed with her on the jungle gym. She had a serious boyfriend, also Cambodian, and on one visit, she invited us to her wedding. It took place in an auditorium on Elizabeth Street in Chinatown. I was amazed at how lavish it was. We sat with young Cambodian women who showed us how and what to eat. The chopsticks were longer than the ones we were accustomed to in Japanese and Chinese restaurants. Our tablemates held them by the tips, far away from the food they were picking up. We ate with chopsticks every week, but we saw that the Cambodian style went beyond our skills.

Sroeun and her groom looked like royalty. Her dress was gold embroidered red satin. Her headdress resembled the peaked, temple-like structures you see in Thai prints. Dish after luscious dish appeared at our table. When people got up to dance, a few young women pulled Tammy into their circle. She did her best to imitate their graceful bends and turns. Their agility with chopsticks was again displayed in the dance. All the joints of their long fingers were articulated in beautiful, stylized patterns.

I wondered how this poor family could afford this opulent wedding. At the end, I got my answer. Everyone emptied their wallets and purses of the big bills they had brought. I did the same, but wished I had been to an ATM a little more recently. After the party, Sroeun and her husband set off for their new home in Lowell, Massachusetts, where he, like so many Cambodian refugees, would work in a microwave plant.

Our lives were not just centered around the city. Tammy and I traveled, not just to North Carolina and Florida, but also to Indiana and Massachusetts. Once we headed to Cape Cod with Mary, my oldest and dearest friend from college. Mary and I sat amazed as Tammy ordered and devoured a huge crab with hairy legs. My picky little eater, who had to be cajoled into pecking at the most meager portion of my cooking, had no trouble ripping the legs from the body and sucking out every last morsel of the meat inside. She didn't enjoy eating so much as the experience of eating. Her favorite foods were artichokes, walnuts that had to be cracked open, and lobsters. Her adventurousness didn't extend to sweets. She hated chocolate all her life. All the bunnies and Cadbury eggs in her Easter baskets ended up on my hips.

We went on fall foliage excursions with Donna, Bob and Mary, where she would have meltdowns followed by deep communion with the forces of nature. Bugs and birds enthralled her. Observing the tug and pull of our relationship, Bob noted that we were each able to compromise. When Donna had baby Ariana, Tammy acquired a new friend.

Karen, she who "no like nobody give her no trouble," taught music at Friends and then went to Sierra Leone in the Peace Corps. The gypsy rightly read her determined stride. Her blond hair bouncing on her shoulders and her confident mien told the story—don't mess with Karen.

When we first met, she invited me over to play Parcheesi. She clobbered me, as she did with every game, and then asked if I would like to hear something. She put on a record and began to sing. I almost fainted from the beauty of her voice. Her one-room apartment was filled to capacity with sound, glorious sound. I could not believe I knew someone who could sing like this.

Turns out she had been the mezzo of an opera company in San Francisco and had toured with the Met National Company.

When she got to the little village far from the cities of Bo and Freetown in Sierra Leone, a posse of kids was waiting and perpetually hung around her dwelling. A six-year-old named Jonathan distinguished himself from the crowd. Over the following two years she grew so fond of Jonathan that she wanted to bring him back to America.

In this culture, woman and mother were one in the same. She was just one more mother for each child. When she went to the woman who she knew to be Jonathan's "real" mother, she asked how she would feel if Jonathan came to the US with her.

"Let him go! Let him learn!" came the enthusiastic reply. But Karen faced steep bureaucratic challenges, which she at last overcame. I would like to see someone stop her once she made up her mind.

Tammy and I went out to Indiana to visit her and Jonathan. Tammy fussed and fumed her way through the Indiana State Fair, demanding every cotton candy she saw. I should have bought it once, but I knew she would hate the sugary stuff.

When she talked back to me, resisting any suggestion, Karen hit the roof. "You don't talk to your mother that way," she exclaimed, and to punctuate her statement she hurled a shoe across the room. Tammy stopped cold, her mouth wide open. Then Karen looked at me and whispered, "Sorry." But I saw that a dose of Karen once in a while would do Tammy a world of good.

Tammy was slow to learn to dress herself. Brushing her teeth never became an automatic habit. Loud shrieks and tantrums accompanied the rituals of bathing and hygiene. Every night she went to bed under the playing loft. Every morning, I woke up with her snuggling by my side

We went to school together and were under the same roof all day. Sometimes I would see her pass by with her class on the way to the gym.

Sometimes we would wave in the cafeteria. After the first few months of hiding in the cubbies, she learned what she was supposed to do. Her teachers the following year had no hint of that particular misconduct. My parents visited her classroom for Grandparents Day. My mother said the teacher let Tammy wander around while everyone else sat in a circle. She said it wasn't right, but I suspected that the teachers didn't want to risk a dramatic fit in front of all the visitors. With the support of the Friends Seminary community, we weathered our lives pretty well. Tammy suddenly broke out with the chicken pox just as final exams were beginning. The school nurse closed her office to sit with Tammy in my apartment while I gave an exam.

I let go of any idea of romance in my life. When a man from the church asked me out, I said I really couldn't leave Tammy. He said that his daughter was an expert baby sitter and would take care of her while we went out to eat. Back from dinner at his apartment, we found his distraught daughter. She had not been able to prevent Tammy from running into the night in this unfamiliar part of Manhattan. I found her immediately, but I told him I just couldn't do it. Truly I didn't care. Only Tammy was on my mind.

Tammy's third grade teacher, Kathy, and Mary Lou, the head of the Lower School requested a parent conference. This was routine and perfunctory. This was my fourth, though in the past I don't remember Mary Lou coming.

We settled ourselves in the little chairs of a lower school classroom, exchanged pleasantries and had a few laughs. Then Mary Lou said, "Marge, you are doing a wonderful job with Tammy," with a look of sympathy bordering on pity. As innocuous as these words were, I felt a sudden pang of foreboding.

"Tammy tries very hard," she continued, "but she is constantly frustrated. She just cannot do what the other kids can do. Right, Kathy?"

Kathy looked down as though reluctant to say anything at all.

"I adapt things for her," she finally said, "but I agree that this will catch up with her in the fourth grade. It will be hard for her."

I had to catch up. I knew that like me, the school believed that support, encouragement, and acceptance could bring around a child who had suffered early emotional trauma. That's why they took Tammy in the first place. Now, what were they thinking?

"She needs a new setting, one that will meet her needs," said Mary Lou.

The air in the room was suddenly too thick to breathe. This was it. Tammy was being counseled out. Tears welled.

With all my attention directed toward getting a grip on my disappointment, I could barely follow the conversation. My most urgent concern was not crying. If only I could beam myself home and avoid the humiliation of my misery. *Please Lord,* I thought, *spare me the indignity of emitting audible sobs in front of my colleagues.*

"Yes, of course," I managed. Having witnessed defensive parents over the years, I knew it was futile to argue. But the hooked fish always wriggles. I wanted to fight. Look how far she's come, I wanted to scream. Look what a worthy little trooper she is. Remember how excited everyone was when she took off reading. She can match pitches. She can imitate rhythms. Look at her gifts in PE.

I sat still in my little chair feeling the fresh ache of banishment, struggling to stifle my tears.

I knew this decision had not been made lightly. My colleagues and I were family. They must have whispered sadly about my foolish denial. They must have had meetings debating how long they could keep her. "It would be better for her to be where she can succeed," I whispered.

"There's a Catholic school in the Bronx that does amazing work with special needs kids," said Mary Lou.

I could barely contain my horror. My Unitarian daughter in a Catholic school? And in the Bronx yet.

I noticed Kathy averting her eyes as I tried to subtly blink back tears. My poor baby. She wasn't going to have a Friends Seminary education. My hope— that her bright peers would pull her up, that these nurturing teachers would throw her a life raft to keep her afloat until she got on the bank with every-one else—wasn't to be. I couldn't wait to get out of there and take her home. *My precious girl. I have failed you.*

"Or you could have her tested and placed by the Board of Ed," said Mary Lou. "Come into my office next week and I'll give you some tips."

"Thank you. I'll do that," I said as got to my feet and rushed to splash water on my face. I felt I could give Tammy no greater gift than an educa-tion in this school. I loved it from the first day I taught there eighteen years earlier. Would she ever again be in a place that believed "there is that of God in every child"? Would anyone ever again see her as a vessel of divinity?

Tammy was leaping and swirling a long satin ribbon when I came to fetch her from the afterschool program. When she saw me, she came running. I wished she were small enough for me to carry home. A few years earlier I could have picked her up and felt consoled by her clutching body. She held my hand as we crossed Stuyvesant Park, but broke away to climb on the statue of Peter Stuyvesant. She pulled herself up in dangerous ways, but I knew she wouldn't fall. She was as lithe as any climbing animal. "Come on, Tammy. You know you aren't supposed to climb on Peg leg Pete."

"I know."

"You remember why?"

"Attractive nuisance," she said. She remembered. Once a cop had been walking through the park and warned her that the statue was not to climb on. Hal had said that the city would be liable if a child got hurt because the statue fell into the category of 'attractive nuisance.'

"I'll take you to the playground where you can climb on the jungle gym."

She was a magical climber. While I watched her, I felt a new solidarity with parents. How painful were the wishes of all mothers and fathers. I thought I would be able to avoid their mistakes but here I was, forced to bury a dream.

PART II
1988-1991

5

PS 40 AND MOM

Out of the secure home of Friends and into the labyrinthine bureaucracy of the New York City Public School System! They tested Tammy, and as usual, she scored in the low average range. But the tester noted some "remarkable utterances." I had often witnessed these surprising flashes and was pleased that they were on the record. One time when we were chatting with my friends after seeing the Broadway show *The Secret Garden*, Tammy piped up, "The real secret garden is their memories of their mothers, Rose and Lily." I wished I'd thought of that.

Her emotional history and her diagnosis from St. Vincent's (not the intelligence testing) indicated that she belonged in MIS 1, Modified Instructional Services 1, the least restrictive of the MIS programs. Our neighborhood elementary school, PS 40, the very school my father had gone to in 1911, had a MIS 1 classroom.

Our fourth summer in North Carolina, my mother's health had deteriorated. The sarcoidosis she had been diagnosed with gave her shortness of breath. One thing led to the next. She took Prednisone to free up her lungs, and it caused such severe osteoporosis that she was in constant pain from fractures to her vertebrae. In an effort to strengthen her bones, the doctor prescribed calcium, but it sometimes stayed dangerously in her blood. To encourage the calcium to enter the bone, my mother had calcitonin shots. We got the nurse up the street to show me how to administer them.

The pain robbed her of her zest to do things. I knew she was failing when she no longer wanted to spend Saturday mornings browsing the yard sales of Kings Mountain with me. She was such a bargain maven that whenever she went into the McGinnis Store downtown, my cousin John would say to the salespeople. "If you can sell that lady anything at full price, you're going to win a trip to Hawaii." Later he would whisper in my ear, "Nobody's gone to Hawaii yet."

Once when we were sitting on the front porch, doing nothing, just catching the evening breeze, my self-assured mother said, "You know, there's something to this women's lib." I was stunned. Could it be that this a total stranger to self-doubt had suffered from Betty Friedan's "problem without a name"? Could she have imagined for herself an alternate life, where her achievements were her own and not just support of my father?

For these summers, my father read, went to Kiwanis, and prepared talks on the Dead Sea Scrolls while Mom and I chatted. There was no time that wasn't good for reminiscing, analyzing Tammy, or gossiping. We talked and laughed while making meals together, watching Tammy play, or taking a walk up the hill. She claimed that fighting gravity would help her bones.

When I was a freshman in college, she went to take some food to a poor family. Upon entering the open door, she found five children and no adults. A baby with no diaper lay in a massively soiled crib. She didn't want to, but she had to report this neglect to the authorities. The children were immediately taken from the home and since there were not enough foster families around, she volunteered to take two tiny girls until a home was found. She brought them when she came for a visit my freshman year at Muhlenberg College. They looked vacant, shell-shocked. I recognized the same look when I met Tammy for the first time. In a few days they were placed, and my parents took their older brother, Burton for the next year. He went to my old elementary school. My brother was living at home, getting a masters at Rutgers. They both seemed happy to have a temporary brother.

Burton was a bright child, but spoiled in the way that neglected children often are. He had not been given normal restrictions and had been free to roam around on his own without telling anyone what he was up to. Mom had some dramatic conflicts with him over just the basic idea that she needed to know where he was. He had a lot of charm and seemed to like to tell me everything when I was home. He was 10 and I was 18. When he was finally placed, he went through a tough period of adjustment.

One night he showed up at the house, having walked about forty miles to get there. He was mute. He wouldn't answer why he had come. It was obvious that this was where he wanted to make his home, but the authorities had to be contacted and he had to go back. He ended up with a lady who collected coins. He came to visit again, but this time with his new mom's blessings. He said, "We're crazy numismatists." My parents kept in touch with him. He turned out to be a responsible citizen – he married and had children. I met him once more when he helped my parents move at the beginning of my father's retirement. They were proud of him. Little wonder that I chose to pull a child out of the system.

More and more, matters of belief seemed insignificant to me. Why get riled about something for which there is no proof? "I never thought you would go for some way-out religion," Mom said, as I took to Unitarianism. I said nothing. It seemed to me that now, when she was getting increasingly ill, would be an unfortunate time to introduce the notion of no afterlife. But it was hubris on my part to think that my thoughts would rattle her. Her faith had nothing to do with anything I might say. As we tap danced about the existence of God, I discovered that she wasn't the narrow-minded literalist I had supposed. With dismay, she asked me, "How can you disregard the source of everything that is?" So that was where she was coming from. I felt that I could meet her here. *God* was a word for the wellspring of being. Practicing the Lutheran faith was just a means of channeling her sense of awe. For her,

I went to the Lutheran Church in Kings Mountain every week and even sang in the choir.

By now, Tammy was an expert bike rider and tooled around the rolling hills of the neighborhood on her own. One day a car pulled into the drive and a man rushed to our door carrying Tammy in his arms. She had had a collision with his pick-up truck. Tammy's head was bleeding, yet she was crying so little that I thought she might be badly hurt. X-rays at Kings Mountain's little hospital showed that this was just one of those mishaps of childhood. She didn't even require stitches. What surprised me in retrospect was that the driver of the pick-up, a complete stranger, knew where she lived and who we were. We weren't in New York any more. I found the loss of anonymity unsettling.

Toward the end of our last summer in Kings Mountain, the summer before Tammy entered PS 40, I got a call that at last my name had come up for a two-bedroom apartment in Stuyvesant Town. I left Tammy in the unsteady hands of my parents to fly to New York to take care of the move. I traded in my view of the ConEd Tower for the stately Empire State. Tammy and I would each have a bedroom. We had a new place to go with the new school.

The first day of Fourth Grade, when I took Tammy to PS 40, just a few short blocks from Friends Seminary, we were turned away because I hadn't brought Tammy's immunization record. We hurried back to Friends to get it from the nurse but by now, I had my own first day of teaching to attend to. When I ran into Michelle, who drove Michael in from New Jersey every day, I said, "I'm desperate. It's her first day in a new school."

"Oh, don't worry about it, Marge. I'll walk Tammy over there. I need to check out this new teacher anyway."

'Of course you do," I said, laughing. "You're saving my life."

I was teaching French II, when Michelle came back and tapped on the window of my door. "Excusez-moi, mes enfants."

I poked my head out. "Well?"

"If I could design a teacher for Tammy, this would be the guy. "

We both jumped up and down.

Ebullient, warm, outspoken, Marty Brynien believed that these children could do anything and set about to making them experts. He became her teacher for the next three years, arguably the most productive years of her life. When they learned about South America, he enlisted the kids to raid their moms' jewelry boxes for Mardi Gras beads and worthless shiny trinkets. Then he lay on the floor and had them outline him on butcher paper. Voilà – Carmen Miranda in the tutti fruiti hat emerged, her neck adorned with copious strings of beads and her hat wound tight with jewels. Posted on the wall she was a sight to behold. Along with Carmen's glorious effigy came knowledge of the countries of South America and their customs and geography.

One day that fall I asked Tammy, "Do you notice much of a difference between the kids at PS 40 and the kids at Friends?"

"Not even close," she said.

"Which do you like better?" I asked.

"Are you kidding?" she said. "Here I'm the smartest kid in the class."

Another topic they studied was the Titanic. Ask Tammy about the Carpathian or the California and she will recount the tragic missteps to this day. My father was visiting us and remembered that he was a second grader, right there at PS 40 in 1912, when the ship went down. Tammy could not wait to tell Mr. Brynien about how her poppop learned of the tragedy from weeping PS 40 teachers.

Mr. Brynien gave homework in abundance. Friends Seminary had asked her to read and keep a log. Mr. Brynien gave page after page of skill-building activities. I saw that Tammy was in a place where she could succeed. Friends students can generally make intuitive leaps. Special Ed kids like Tammy need to feel their way step by step.

Once when Tammy was sick, I came by to get work for her. Mr. Brynien insisted that the class greet me politely. My entrance became a lesson in manners. I asked 38-year-old Tammy how she would compare Friends Seminary and PS 40.

—A school's a school.

—What about Mr. Brynien.

—He's a nice teacher. I learned more in his class than in any class I think I've ever had. Cuz he wasn't afraid to actually teach. Some of the schools that I went to with special needs kids, they were afraid. *Oh, you shouldn't teach them so much because they got special needs. They're not going to be able to learn it.* But he wasn't afraid to just say *you know what? I'm just going to teach you about certain things whether you understand it or not. At least you'll have it in case down the road* oh now I get what the person was saying about that.
He taught us about the Titanic, Tutankhamen, Egypt and Carmen Miranda. OMG he actually dressed up in a tutti frutti hat. Everybody was like *oh hell no!* You see a guy with a mustache wearing a tutti frutti hat same kind as Carmen had. We were like *what the hell did he take?* He was pretty out there sometimes. Mr. Sachs came in and he had this weird look and was like *OK I'm going to leave.* I mean he opens the door and sees Mr. Brynien in the tutti frutti hat.

It had apples, bananas, pineapples, oranges. He's in like this weird looking dressy kind of thing that should have been on a female, and he's shakin' and shakin' and singing the song she sang in the movie. Mr. Sachs comes in, looks at him. Of course his back is turned to Mr. Sachs. He looks at him, he goes *Okay* –walks right out, so that should have told you right there. I guess he thought *OK, the guy's a little wacko. Let me come back when he's had some caffeine or something.* I mean Mr. Sach's face was like floored, like *what the heck is this guy doing with a girlie outfit with a bunch of fruit on his head?*

I was laughing. I was encouraging her. Shame on me. I'd lay odds that Mr. Brynien never taught a single lesson in his life in a dress, with or without caffeine. And Mr. Sachs? He was a vice principal at the junior high. He probably never even met Mr. Brynien. This is why I trained myself never to believe anything Tammy said. Trouble is that sometimes she was telling the truth.

Fortunately, Tammy's Christmas break coincided with mine, and we went to Florida for what turned out to be my mother's last Christmas. We could see that she was ailing. The steroid-induced osteoporosis had gotten worse. She sat very still, dreading the moment when she would have to move. I gave her an audio book of Russell Baker's *Growing Up*. She lay in bed, listening to it. She said it brought back her own childhood, playing barefoot on the red Carolina clay.

Gone was the effervescence with which she had graced the steps of St. Peter's all the years of my father's ministry there. She welcomed, she greeted, she drew out and told stories. My father was the brains and metaphysics; she was the heart and humanity. She came to Margie and Joey's bedside at night and listened to their joys and woes and then commissioned them to say their prayers. Her temper was fierce. One time I came home to find all the clutter and tangle of my untended room strewn on the roof outside my window and all through the backyard. She was constantly infuriated by my slovenliness, yet if she wanted to understand it, she needed to look no farther than my father's desk. The fourth of twelve children, yet the first girl, she had had her fill of child rearing before she got married. Two children seemed like nothing to her. She went from president of the PTA at Jefferson School to president of the PTA at Plainfield High. When I was in the sixth grade she went back to school at Westminster Choir College and then taught solfege and piano to my friends.

As usual that Christmas, I left Tammy with her while I went to buy out ToysRUs. As usual my mother commissioned me to buy a necklace or some earrings so that Tammy would have a Christmas gift for me. "Tammy must learn to give," she said. For the first time Tammy gave her trouble. "I didn't get this, Nana. You did."

"True, Tammy. I was helping you out. Next year, you remember to get Mommy something."

My mother once commented that Elijah went up to heaven on a chariot of fire with an assist from a blazing whirlwind. Not one to criticize the Almighty, she did venture, "Now wouldn't that be a better way?" She died that March leaving my father to fend for himself. The congregation sang "For All the Saints who from their Labors Rest."

6

THE HOSPITAL

We were passing through the waiting room at St Vincent's after Tammy's therapy session, when a staff member came by with a bunch of helium-filled balloons for a birthday party. *No, no,* I thought. *Not balloons.* Plump and colorful, they thrilled Tammy the way a rich vein excites a prospector. Eager to stake her claim, she reached up to grasp them. I put my arms around her and held her tight. "No Tammy. Those balloons belong to somebody else. You can't take them."

At first she moaned and strained to seize her precious treasure. But then, frustrated by my snug hold, she set to wailing in desperation at the top of her lungs.

"Cut it out, Tammy," I said. She was a fourth grader, almost ten. How could this be happening?

She screamed all the louder. The noise she made was so alarming that therapists up and down that hall emerged from their little rooms to respond to what sounded like a dire crisis.

"Sorry," I said, shouting a little myself to be heard over the shrieks. "She really likes balloons."

Tammy's therapist, Gerry, came running to help me calm her down. Another therapist said, "Gerry, this behavior is very regressed."

Gerry said, "Come on Tammy. Just relax."

Another therapist said, "This is 18-month-old behavior."

Another said, "This child should be hospitalized."

A consensus started to form that Tammy should be put in the pediatric psychiatric ward immediately. It was an emergency. Her behavior was so aberrant that she needed a therapeutic setting.

"What do you think, Gerry?" I asked, still holding firm my struggling, screaming nine-year old.

"It's something we haven't tried. I don't want to send her home like this."

"When she's away from the balloons she'll be all right."

I knew from experience this was true. She was tenacious enough to give her all to acquiring what she wanted, but she would let it go if I could just get her out of there. Though this frenzy looked like utter loss of control, I knew Tammy was trying to see if it would work. Every inoculation she had ever had required the cocoon – restraint inside a kiddie straight-jacket. The sight of the needle sent her into the altered state of a demonic dervish. But as soon as the big guys slapped the cocoon on her, the screaming tizzy totally subsided. "If she were a true phobic," they said, "she would keep on fighting."

I wanted to get her out of there and go home, but all these professionals were saying that her tiny-tot behavior needed treatment. I should let her get some attention at the hospital. I was swayed, and I was exhausted. I knew that she would return to "normal" without a hospital, but then I thought, maybe they knew something. Maybe they could figure out how to prevent these episodes of high drama. On top of everything, in two days I was supposed to be the emcee at a big event to celebrate the tenure of our principal who was leaving the school. I always had Tammy with me by myself. A stay at St Vincent's might do us both some good.

I checked her in and went home to work on my jokes. I sat down to write but was overcome with a feeling of anxious loneliness. I missed her and couldn't imagine that she was not feeling bereft in that bleak locked ward. When I left, she was crying and I heard the door click. That worry I felt at Donna and Bob's wedding stalked me.

I tried to focus on Joyce, our principal. She had worked miracles in the school. But jokes were in the imperfections. One time she went out into Third Avenue and 86th Street at 4 AM and determined that the snow looked bad. She called a snow day. By 8AM, the sun was shining brightly. After that, for ten years, we never had a snow day again. I wrote that there were certain vocabulary deficiencies in the school. "Do you know," I wrote, "that there are children –teenagers even—who don't know the meaning of 'snow day'?" That should get a chuckle.

I thought of the first time Tammy had a meltdown over balloons. It was when she turned six. Her brothers Matt and Martin came over for cake and ice cream. As they left, I gave them each a balloon. Tammy stomped her feet and screamed. The whole building must have wondered what torture I was inflicting on her. The next day, a colleague said to me, "Marge, you have to realize that for a child, balloons are something of value." At six, maybe.

As soon as school let out, I went to visit Tammy. I had signed her away for two weeks. It was only at this visit that I understood what they did there. They used "behavior modification" techniques – if she disobeyed a rule, she was put in a padded room until she calmed down. This was supposed to teach her how to control herself. In the visiting room, there was a little black boy about Tammy's age whose visitor was a white priest. As Tammy played with a puzzle, the priest told the boy that God was everywhere.

"What everywhere?" said the startled kid.

The priest smiled benevolently. "Yes, He's right here."

The boy asked, "You're telling me that God is in this room? I don't see him."

"Ah," said the priest, "He's not visible, but He is here."

"Is he there?" said the boy, pointing to an empty space.

"Yes," said the priest.

"Then, let me at him," said the child with surprising heat, putting up his dukes.

Tammy wandered over to another family across the room, a mother, a teen-age son, and the small girl who was hospitalized.

The monitor said, "Tammy, you have to stay with your mother. That's one of the rules. You stay with the person who is visiting you."

"Oh that's okay," said the other mother. "She's not bothering us."

"Well, Tammy has to obey the rules."

The monitor tried to lead her back to me. I saw that Tammy was going to be taken to task for not visiting with me. "It's okay," I said. "She probably wants to get to know the other little girl."

"This is a rule."

"Okay. Come here, Tammy."

Tammy began to kick up a fuss. I wondered if she was mad at me for putting her here. The burly man was summoned, and he took her away. I could hear her screaming in the padded room. They said she would probably be there a while and I should go home.

On the crosstown bus back to Stuyvesant Town, I thought of the Milgram experiment at Yale, where volunteers thought they were inflicting painful shocks to students in order to increase learning. The students were really actors, pretending to experience pain as the volunteers administered the fake electrical impulses. The volunteers, really the subjects of the experiment, sometimes inflicted what appeared to be intense pain. Apparently, they did it because they believed the white-coated professionals, who told them that they would ruin the experiment if they stopped. I always wondered what I would have done.

I remembered discussing this with my friend and mentor Annette. Her family had been devastated by the Holocaust, and she herself had survived a camp.

"Oh no, darling," she said. "I know what I would have done."

I knew it too. She would have walked out of there before the first jolt was administered. I wished I had her moral compass.

Now it was a question not of some stranger but of Tammy. I felt like the hapless experiment subject, just blindly obeying the white coats. My own judgment told me this was a terrible mistake, that this locked ward was not therapeutic in any way. It was distressing for no apparent reason. The bus passed University Place where Tammy and I would have gone for sushi after her therapy session. She would have savored salmon roe and flying fish eggs and even eaten the edible nasturtiums, noting, as always, that they didn't taste like much.

I went to the big event the next day with my sad attempts at humor on 3X5 cards. Hundreds of people were in the Meeting House to fete our out-going head. A decade earlier she had saved the school from disaster, leading an institution in turmoil into a new healthy era where the admissions department was flooded with applicants. She adored being in front of large groups and used the word "wonderful" with comical frequency.

I was to emcee what was staged as a graduation; only there was just one graduate. This was the class of Joyce McCray.

I introduced myself as a teacher who had been there for twenty years.

"You know," I said, "I have learned a lot from Joyce. For instance, she taught me to listen to the students. Listening—it's really a great idea. You know what a student told me the other day? That where her dad works, people get a gold watch after twenty years."

This sympathetic crowd had come to party; they found this uproarious. I was on a roll. Tammy and the hospital vanished from my consciousness. By the time I compared Joyce's festivities for the bi-centennial of the school to the modest (by comparison) celebration of the bi-centennial of the French Revolution, the meetinghouse was ringing with laughter.

Then Susie Cohen came out. She had gone through the school from kindergarten to graduation. A lifer. Now she was a grown-up teacher. When she was in the fifth grade, how she wanted to learn French! On her second day in French she wrote a skit and brought in a sock puppet to perform it. The poor sock was pretty much stuck at "Bonjour." Dressed like Joyce and wearing a wig that made her look like Joyce, she tossed off a Joyce-like monologue liberally sprinkled with "wonderfuls," each of which brought down the house.

After the event, during which more than one speaker noted that if Marge Gonzalez wanted a gold watch, she took the wrong job, there was a reception in the courtyard. I ran into Tammy's pediatrician, who had kids in the school.

"Tammy is in the pediatric psychiatric ward at St. Vincent's," I told her. I thought I saw a troubled shadow cross her face.

"What for?" she asked.

"They seem to think they can help her act more on her own her age level."

"Oh," she said, with a strained smile.

I've got to spring Tammy from that place, I thought.

Going west on the bus to St. Vincent's, I had another crosstown rumination. I thought of Sartre and his gloss on the story of Abraham and Isaac. The Old Testament God was some sadist, I thought, telling Abraham to sacrifice his son. For me, the fact that the angel stopped him in time didn't really do much to diminish the cruelty. Now Abraham knew what evil he was capable of. Anyway, Sartre's point was that Abraham had to decide for himself if the voice was God's. Maybe it belonged to the great trickster. In the end, it was all up to Abraham –no palming it off on a higher power. If a voice told me to hurt Tammy, I would assume that I had suddenly developed schizophrenia.

So there was my Tammy, tough in a way, but to me, fragile, damaged, in need of love, of a soft route to progress toward restoring her basic trust in people. How do you get over rejection by your parents, your first line of defense against the harshness of the world? I believed in nothing in the meta-physical realm, yet I was an acolyte of the power of love. This "behavior mod" was divorced from love. It was more like dog training, only instead of treats for good performance, there was the padded room for bad performance. Who knows – maybe it could prevent tantrums, but the manner was completely external. Results without insight. Like Abraham, I had to decide what was best, and for me, a home where she was beloved beyond measure beat out this bleak, rule-driven, impersonal institution by a mile.

I told the secretary that I wanted to take Tammy home. She reminded me that I had signed up for two weeks.

"I changed my mind," I said.

"Well, you'll have to talk to Dr. Finn.*"

Dr. Finn was the psychiatrist in charge. There was always a psychiatrist in charge, usually a male, and then a whole group of therapists (social workers like Gerry or psychologists or licensed health care professionals). Only psychiatrists could prescribe meds. The clinic always reminded me of a chicken coop with one rooster and a passel of hens.

Dr. Finn was young and maybe because I was living such an ascetic life, he seemed kind of sexy. He reminded both Tammy and me of Jimmy Smits.

"Dr. Finn, I want to take Tammy home."

"She's here for two weeks."

She was still only my foster child, but I was in charge. I had custody.

"I don't think it's working."

"You haven't given it enough time."

Okay, I was in charge.

"I'd like to take her home."

"She needs to be here."

"This room she is put in feels like a punishment and not a therapeutic, learning thing," I said.

He looked at me with contempt. "Maybe you would like to run the clinic."

Whoa, I thought. Maybe you should learn to be a shrink. I had to get her out of here *tout de suite*.

"I want Tammy released as soon as possible."

He had to do it.

I met Tammy in the visiting room. "Guess what. You're going home."

"Can we stop for sushi?" Either she was really hungry, or she was indeed on the spectrum.

On Monday, Joyce happened to be having lunch at my table in the cafeteria. I told her about Dr. Finn and his snarky comment.

"Ha," she said. "You should have told him 'No thanks. I already have a much better job than running your crummy clinic.'"

7

RESPITE

I went to a meeting of Single Mothers by Choice, billed as a support group with childcare provided. Tammy was the only child who showed up except for a sleeping infant or two. She quickly found the blocks.

The women sat in a circle. Some were thinking of having a baby or adopting while others were pregnant by accident or by sperm donor. As they described their situations, a sharp divide emerged. One of the pregnant women, who looked chic and intelligent, said, "I am going to have amniocentesis. I want to know if this child is defective. If it has Down syndrome or something like that, I plan to abort."

Several chimed in that they would do likewise. One said, "It's enough for me to raise a child by myself. I can't deal with a Down syndrome kid."

I could hear Tammy in the other room fussing in her high-pitched voice. I could tell she was protesting some restriction or other. I felt for the caretaker.

Another woman, dressed for comfort in loose stretchy sweat clothes, said that she had gone out of her way to adopt Down syndrome children. "Here you are threatening to kill your child if it's not perfect. I can tell you that Down syndrome kids are loving and devoted. What do you want from a child?"

The group was quiet.

Finally I broke the silence. "I got a school-age child out of foster care," I said, "mainly because I didn't have the money to take off from work or pay a sitter while I taught. You can hear her in the next room. For me this was a good move. I didn't produce a child – I took a child who really needed a home.

I looked at the pictures in the foster care files. There are so many children being thrown away, growing up unwanted."

"Good for you," said the chic pregnant woman. "But I don't want to save the world. I just want to beat out my biological clock."

So, I thought, she just needs to fulfill her evolutionary destiny to keep her genes in play. What a crazy species we are. We'll take in dogs that need homes but let the young of our own species languish in limbo so we can produce replicas of ourselves. Then I remembered that I would have done the same if I could have afforded it. Oh well, necessity had pushed me onto the moral high ground and willy-nilly that's where I was. But nothing like the serial adopter of Down syndrome kids. She occupied the moral pinnacle.

Seeing an impasse, the facilitator said, "Well, we all have equally valid reasons for our choices. Let me turn to the topic for today – respite. What about respite? Have any of you thought about how you will take the occasional break from caring for your child?"

The conversation veered off in the new direction. "Thank goodness my mother wants to help me with the baby. She's my backup," said one of the pregnant women.

"I would really like to find out what resources there are," said the woman with the Down syndrome children. "That's one of the reasons I came here. I'm wondering if there is a place where you can take the kids for a few days."

"Wait a minute," said the chic lady. "You chose to have those kids. Why don't you want to be with them?" *Chic and bitchy,* I thought. Any pooch she brought home would have to come with papers.

"Just because I chose them doesn't mean I don't get tired. They have laundry. They need meals. They need help eating. I shouldn't get tired just because I chose them?"

I was tired too. My mother had helped me with Tammy, but now she was gone. There was no one else. I thought I had better get some respite too. It sounded like a tantrum in there.

Tammy was going to camp. There was a charter bus waiting in a mall parking lot to take the special needs group to Camp Huntington in High Falls, New York, for a whole month. Tammy and I climbed into our rented car for the ride to Yonkers.

"You're going to have fun, Tammy," I said.

"Uh-huh."

"Are you excited?"

"No."

"I'll write. By the way, I *am* excited. I'm going to take a trip."

"Don't forget to bring me a momentum."

"Sure, I'll bring you a memento."

We found the bus, surrounded by families who all belonged to my club, the club of people with kids who are different. Some had physical disabilities; others had cognitive and emotional issues. I was happy to have found a place where kids with PDD were welcome. A counselor with a clipboard checked them off as they got on the bus.

"Try to get a window seat so I can wave to you," I said.

"Okay. Bye, Mom."

When the bus was loaded, it took off with the throng waving and calling, "Have fun!" "Have a great time!" "We'll miss you!"

As soon as the bus turned out into the road, the mood changed to raucous celebration. A cheer went up. People yelled, "Four weeks of freedom!" "Praise the Lord!" Hands waved in the air. I heard a hallelujah or two.

On the plane to Paris, I thought about Tammy. How could she sleep without the usual medley of lullabies? Would they know how to handle her meltdowns? Then I thought of Donna's brother, his saying, "You know, kids are pretty resilient." She loved everything there—swimming, arts and crafts, singing. Discipline yourself, Marge. Let her go have fun. Go have fun yourself. That's the point of respite.

My father, now in his eighties and still mourning my mother, would join me the next day. He could not rest from travel, I guess. While Anne, a fellow French teacher at Friends, and I took an NYU course about how the architecture of Paris appears in literature, he was going on a tour all around France. We had planned to spend a few days together in Paris before his trip.

As I was settling into our hotel room, I turned on the TV. There were *The Golden Girls* dubbed in French. "Bea Arthur speaks French. Who knew?" I said to nobody. Then I set out for Montmartre. I always loved the view. It was one of my favorite haunts when I lived in Paris for a year as a student. Nothing much had changed on the subways except that the *portillon automatique* no longer closed you out as the train was entering the station.

I took the little funicular up the hill. The lights of Paris were coming on as I reached the broad steps in front of Sacré-Coeur. Before me stretched one of the most beautiful and celebrated views in the world. I could spot the Eiffel Tower and Notre Dame. The panorama before me signaled a future I had stopped anticipating. But there it was, alive with tiny lights, a new vista opening up like the shimmering city before me. If camp worked out I would survive Tammy's childhood. Don't cry for me Argentina – I had unlocked the secret of child rearing: summer camp.

My dad arrived on schedule. It had never occurred to me that he would outlive my mother. She was six years younger and had a more robust constitution. Nonetheless, here was this frail, stooped old man going on with his life on his own. His eyes sparkled with the excitement of seeing something new. In German "debt" and "guilt" are the same word. I felt equal measures of both. He imparted to me his love of books, scholarship, and language.

But on the guilt side, I had much to atone for. I had been nastier to this gentle soul than to any other human. Mild and kind, he never stopped me. He waited for me to come around. Perhaps I finally had. If life were fair, if there were some overarching karma, the horridness Tammy directed at me was just deserts.

"So what do you want to do in Paris, Daddy?"

"There are a few places in Paris that I've never seen. Have you been to catacombs or St. Denis?"

"Strange to say, I've never been to either one." When I was a student, every weekend I followed a walking tour from the Guide Michelin. How remarkable that my father was the one who would show me something new in Paris.

The catacombs were filled with victims of plagues, wars, and I guess just ordinary old age. They contained the bones of six million. How my father could bear the sight of this necropolis I do not know. Room after dank room was filled with skeletons and skulls, a danse macabre in repose. I felt the chill more than he did. *Memento mori*, I thought, which reminded me that Tammy told me to be sure to bring her some momentums. My little queen of the malapropism, thanks for cheering me up.

As we walked back to the metro, my father noticed the sign, "Visitez les égoux." "What's that?" he asked.

"I believe it's an invitation to visit the scenic sewers of Paris."

"That should be interesting."

"Are you kidding me?" My father's enthusiasm for new experiences knew no bounds.

The sewers turned out to smell even worse than you might imagine. "Don't fall out of the boat, Daddy."

"Don't worry."

As we went to the restaurant by our hotel, I said, "A great day in Paris – first death then decay."

"A truly great day," he agreed, without irony.

The next day we took the metro up to the northern suburb St Denis. The Basilica of Saint-Denis was a revelation. Designated the first Gothic structure ever, it housed the tomb of nearly every king of France from the 10th to the 18th century. This historic treasure trove rejuvenated my father. It reminded me of our first trip to Europe when I was twelve years old. He emerged from Santa Pudenziana in Rome looking like a successful seeker of the Holy Grail.

"What did you think, Daddy?"

"Oh, boy!"

He went off on the bus for ten days, and Anne and I settled into the apartment a French friend had loaned us. At an outdoor café Anne got the *assiette de charcuterie* (cold cuts only of course much better), and I got the *assiette de crudités* (raw things – the grated celery root—to die for).

"Anne, this is so amazing. I'm not worrying. How can this be?" I said.

"Well, Marge, you really did need a break."

"Well this is the ultimate. Have you ever been to the flea market here? There's another place I've never been."

"I'm dying to go to the Musée d'Orsay."

"Okay let's go. I can't wait to see all those paintings that used to be in the Jeu de Paume. Let's do it all."

In the course, I learned about how Paris was turned upside down for more than a decade by the efforts of Napoleon III and Haussmann. Before that the Champs-Elysees was pretty much a sewer and smelled like the charming *égoux* we visited. What emerged was the Paris we know with tree-lined avenues and boulevards and the magnificent Paris Opera House. We saw how the changes in the city altered the backdrop of a national literature. My soul was restored.

When I went to meet my father after his tour, his fellow tourists wanted to be sure I heard how they enjoyed having him along.

"I only hope that when I'm that age, I have half as much curiosity," a gentleman in his fifties told me. I thought of Tennyson's Ulysses again. "I will drink life to the leas." That was my father.

In New York, I rented a car and my dad and I drove up to get Tammy in High Falls. How she had grown! Sunlight had streaked her hair, which fell down her back in a fat braid. I gave her a T-shirt with a shiny Eiffel Tower, purchased at Paris's enormous flea market; she handed me a beautiful macramé necklace and said, "I had fun."

8

TAMMY'S NAMING AND MOTHER OF THE YEAR

Once in a while I wrote to HRS in Miami to remind them that Tammy was with me and that we were waiting for the go ahead for me to adopt her. They ignored me until winter 1990, when a letter informed me that parental rights for Tammy had been terminated and that she was now eligible for a Special Needs Adoption, which would allow her to keep Medicaid and me to still receive the $240 a month I got as a foster mother. The little kindergartener was now a fifth grader.

"Tammy, I can adopt you. We'll change your name from Shaughnessy to Gonzalez." About time.

"That's good," she said, barely looking up from her Barbies. "Only then I won't have the same name as my brothers."

"Hmm. I thought of that too, but Tammy Lynn Shaughnessy Gonzalez is kind of a long name. I'm thinking of something, though. Do you remember when we saw Karate Kid II?"

"Oh, yeah. "

"Remember how we talked about smushing together Tammy and Lynn and calling you Tamlyn, like Tamlyn Tomito? That way we could keep Shaughnessy as a middle name." I'd gotten this idea when I saw the actress's name on the credits.

"Tamlyn Shaughnessy Gonzalez. Yeah."

Thank goodness she bought into the idea of "Tamlyn." Here was a name she could grow into. "Tammy" brought back to me the breathy voice of Debby

Reynolds singing "Tammy's in Love" and a ditsy Sandra Dee. "Tammy Lynn" would work if she had a gig at the Grand Ole Opry, but really, to me, it wasn't a grown-up name. It was certainly not a name I would have given a girl. If it had been up to me, I would have named her "Miranda." (Oh brave new world!) But she came as "Tammy." And as usual, my part was to tinker with what was already set.

Tammy Duckworth and Tammy Baldwin have proved me wrong, I guess, but I was always happy that my name was Margaret. The name had dignity. Even if I went by Marge, a name appropriate for a housewife complaining about waxy buildup, I could fall back on Margaret on occasions that called for solemnity. So now she would have a first name to fall back on, too.

Although Gonzalez is a name so common in New York that the drycleaner asked me for two initials, it is my name. I resented the stubborn inertia of HRS. Tammy had been abandoned over and over. Why not let me adopt her so that she would have the same last name as her mother? Why let her linger in nagging insecurity from kindergarten to fifth grade? Why did they not grasp that name is the basic marker for family? Her name should have been mine all along.

"Don't call me Tammy. Call me Tamlyn."

"Okay, Tamlyn. Sounds like a perfect moniker."

"I was talking to Barbie."

"What about me?"

"You can call me Tammy or Tamlyn."

After we made it official in court, I wanted to celebrate. In the Unitarian Church there is no baptism, but there is something called a Dedication and Naming Ceremony. "Tammy, Tamlyn, let's have a party. You're an official member of the family, so let's celebrate!"

"Sure, if you want to."

"We could have a Naming Ceremony in church, and then everyone could come over for lunch and a party."

"Okay."

"We'll invite Uncle Joe and Aunt Sharon, some of your friends, and some Friends Seminary friends. Deal? You'll help me make the food?"

"Okay."

About that time, I noticed that *Town and Village*, the weekly for Stuyvesant Town and Peter Cooper Village was holding a contest for *Mother of the Year*. I wanted this. *Mother of the Year*-it sounded like the biggest honor possible. Hadn't I knocked myself out for this kid? Hadn't I endured bureaucracies and prejudice? And more. What about the kid herself? She fought me on every front. She didn't want to get in the tub, she didn't want to get out of the tub, she didn't want to sleep. When I rocked her, she refused to close her eyes. If I was on the phone, she made loud fussy noises. And her hair! As straggly and thin as mine was, hers was thick and luxurious. But would she brush it? She would not. Would she let me brush it? No. She left it to tangle and mat until large chunks had to be cut out. She smashed the glass on the picture I had taken of her with me and my parents, and then poked out our eyes.

Sometimes it seemed to me that she was possessed. If an exorcist had been handy I would have consulted with him. She would not eat; she would not speak intelligible words. She would stomp about, her face a drawn mask of fury. When she looked at me, it was with eyes full of rage. She kept it up. If I reached out to her, she pulled away in a jerk of repulsion. I would lie on my bed and think, *I have to kill her.* Her wretchedness was more than a person could bear. Nothing seemed worse than the hell she was enduring. I saw no other remedy for the loud outbursts of infantile anger followed by surly feet stamping and an anorexia far removed from the perfection- seeking anorexia I knew about. Then I would think about how I would have to kill myself.

There was no way I could kill her and then go on living. So there we were, trapped.

But something would finally happen before I came up with a M.O. for the murder/suicide. I would say, "Sushi," and there would be a tiny break in the clouds. I invented sushi therapy, and it was the most effective therapy she ever had. If I could get her to a Japanese restaurant, she would eat a few flying fish eggs and begin to let go of the demons.

And balloons. St. Vincent's was just one event in a series. She treated balloons like gold. Heaven help us if the stupid helium container got away into the sky. She was inconsolable. The whole world had to know. I thought she would convert to Hari Krishna once when she danced along their float on Fifth Avenue. As the parade ended, the indefatigable dancers gave over their huge bunch of balloons to the dancing imp. There must have been twenty-five or thirty balloons attached to that little hand. What I saw were twenty-five potential meltdowns. And there was so much more I don't want to even think about. The tantrums in stores or on street corners before the WAIT sign changed to WALK, the violent refusals to ever leave the playground, the enuresis, the encopresis. Hell yes! I deserved a prize.

"Tammy, they're having a contest for Mother of the Year. If you wrote a letter and sent it in, maybe your letter would win."

"No."

"It won't take long." I sat her at the table with paper and a pen.

"I don't want to."

"You don't want your own mother to be Mother of the Year?"

Deep sighs. "What would I write?"

"Whatever you want. Tell them how you just finally got adopted."

Whining sound, and then a high-pitched wail. "I don't want to!"

"Come on. You can do it, and if you win, we get lots of prizes."

"You mean YOU get lots of prizes." Her voice had descended to its normal sardonic pitch. I was going to win this one – not the prize – but she was going to write. I had filled out many forms about her mental health over the years. They always asked the question, "Does he/she agree and then fail to comply?" I finally asked, "What about a child that says 'no' and then complies." "Oh," they said. "That's normal."

"Just write."

"Don't have much of a choice."

Grumbling and kicking her chair leg, the hostage with a gun to her head began to write.

> Dear Town and Village,
>
> My mom is a very nice, kind and generous person. She loves and caere about me very much. That is why I like her. She is all that I have left of a family that loves me. I hope you feel the same way I feel. I was a foster child now she adopted me March 8 1990 and I love her for that.
>
> PS Here's my address 561 E 14th St ny, New York 10009 apt 10-H Phone number (212) 677-4371 person Margaret Gonzalez.

FROM

Tamlyn
Gonzalez

"Here. Happy?"

"Very happy. Thank you, Sweetheart."

She thrust her note into my hand and stalked off to her room. Sweeter than I expected, but it didn't have a prayer. The "T" of Tamlyn was about as big as the whole rest of the message put together. What a shame. The prizes included a $50 gift certificate for the supermarket, dinner for two at the Stuyvesant Town Café ("the finest in Continental cuisine"), brunch for two at Pete's Tavern (a truly storied Mecca), a waffle iron from Vercesi Hardware and much much more. I usually bought frozen waffles, but I could give the real thing a try.

The whole village that it takes to raise a child turned out for the Naming and Dedication Ceremony. Many teachers from Friends came as well as old friends like Donna and Bob. Judy, my illustrator for my text, *Louis Souris*, brought her husband and two kids from Short Hills. I selected a reading, the famous quote of the Skin Horse in *The Velveteen Rabbit*. "When a child loves you for a long, long time, not just to play with, but REALLY loves you, then you become Real," a nice metaphysical point accessible to the young. I chose *The Velveteen Rabbit* because of its emphasis on relationship, on the power of commitment and love. I wanted us to be a real mother-daughter duo. As much as I wanted to be Tammy's real mother, I wanted her to be my real daughter.

Tammy stood up in front in the church with my brother, sister-in-law, niece and me and smiled out at the congregation, the perfect recipient of this community welcome. She looked grave and determined as the minister touched her forehead with a rose, commissioning her to serve all humanity.

I was thinking that she defied the characteristics of the spectrum. Her kindergarten teacher had noted her joyous exuberance. Last Christmas she said she wanted "A black Barbie." I had always thought black girls should have black dolls and white children should have white dolls. But Tammy insisted that her white Barbies needed black friends. I was proud of her inclusive view of friendship.

These characteristics make her sound normal – even exceptional. But she was odd. Though her differences were not always obvious, she did not behave like other children. I used to say to my mother's ghost, if you were right and you are still there somewhere, could you tweak her brain. Touch it and fix it. Just a smidge.

The minister read a passage from Khalil Gibran:

Your children are not your children.
They are the sons and daughters of Life's longing for itself.
They come through you but not from you,
And though they are with you yet they belong not to you.

This one hadn't even come through me. I had been her mother for six years and I couldn't say for sure if any of the changes in her came from me or were just the ordinary result of the passage of years. The text contained the hard lesson that Tammy often reminded me of. So many times, she has said to me, "I'm not you."

At the party, the kids congregated in her room while the grownups schmoozed everywhere else. I had shopped at green grocers up and down Fourteenth Street and found enough ripe avocados to serve everyone a half with a creamy mixture of scallops and shrimp in the place where the pit used to be. Old friends and new celebrated with us amid the bright bouquets of tulips. Someone gave Tammy a silver bracelet with her new name engraved on it. She received books about adopted kids and the family of man, and lots of jewelry. If she wasn't charming and gracious, no one told me about it.

About a month later, we came home and found the phone ringing. I caught it in time. It was Hal saying, "Who is the greatest mother in the *Town and Village* community? There are, according to the many letters received during the past few weeks, literally hundreds. But though a difficult task it was, the field was narrowed down to only one. Congratulations Margaret Gonzalez."

"Oh my God. It's in the paper?"

"Yup."

"Tammy! I mean Tamlyn! Your letter won!" She didn't respond.

"What else does it say?" I asked Hal.

"It's a nice long piece and it actually shows Tammy's letter."

"Oh my God – well then there you are." Victory!

No sooner did I hang up than the phone rang with a call from *Town and Village*. "We just want to let you know that Tamlyn's letter won hands down. We all sat around and read them and everyone wanted hers to win. So we'll be getting in touch with you to interview you and Tamlyn. Congratulations! We hope you enjoy all the prizes."

We had waffles for breakfast that weekend.

9

BODY IN SPACE

My life at Friends was evenly divided between the two Annettes. Annette Lehu was my mentor. She was the department chair who hired me. The only close French friend I have ever had, she was my window into French culture. In 1940, I was a baby and she was a twenty-year-old in Paris with one Jewish parent and one Catholic parent. When the Nazis came, they took her family away for good. Annette managed to survive. One summer, a few weeks after I returned from a trip to Europe, she called me. "Oh, you're back," she said.

"Yes. I've been back a week or so."

"And you didn't call me?" Her voice was full of pain and anger.

I had no idea I was supposed to call her. This was the beginning of my understanding of what our friendship meant to her. Why me? I don't know. She loved me like a daughter.

One Monday, we were having our morning coffee in the cafeteria. The day before an article on happiness had appeared in the *New York Times* magazine.

"So," I said," what do you think happiness is, Annette?"

She gave me a jaunty smile and sipped her coffee. "Being here, having coffee with you."

The other Annette, Annette Kahn, was the first French teacher we hired after Annette Lehu retired and I became department chair. A tiny Tammy came to her job interview. Annette Kahn contended that she knew why we had hired her. "You wouldn't have to change the stationary." Indeed, Kahn and Lehu looked surprisingly similar in certain scripts.

One time, Annette Kahn and I were packing up our papers for the weekend. 'What do you know about this guy Gardner?" I asked.

"I heard he's pretty good," said Annette. "He's from Harvard, at least"

The next day, Friday, the students had the day off so that the teachers could go to a conference at a mid-town hotel where Gardner would be speaking.

"Well, he's bound to be better than some of the infamous Faculty Enrichment Day speakers from the past," I said, "before you were here. You would not believe some of the . . . I can't say. It's too terrible."

"Oh no you don't," said Annette. "Come on."

"Okay, here's one. A team of experts came to tell us to play a version of Simon Says where nobody is ever out." I thought of how Annette and I frequently played Simon Says in French with beginning students to teach them the parts of the body. Of course we called it *Simon Dit*. "Apparently irreparable harm is done to self-esteem if you're out."

"What?"

"Well, if a kid is out, he feels bad. Feeling bad is BAD, so being out just won't work. Whether you put your hands behind your back when Simon says to or whether you don't, makes no difference. You are not out, and, darn, you feel good. I'm OK, you're OK."

"Did they explain why anyone would want to play such a game?"

"They left that out. The kids missed an entire day of school so the teachers could learn that it doesn't matter if you do things right or if you do them wrong. No kidding. The whole faculty was led in a rollicking game of Simon Says, and we were never out. That's why we esteem ourselves so much. Poor you – you weren't there. This may explain why I'm more arrogant than you."

"I'll match you for arrogance in any field. My scarves are way better than yours, for instance."

"Ooo, got me." Her scarves really were great. "Here's another one from another year– worse than egalitarian Simon Says. We were admonished to love each other. Hugging was recommended."

"Oh, no. Not the touchy-feely era."

"Oh, yes – and an old letch from the math department took to the message immediately."

"Oh, Lord."

"Oh, yes. The under forty crowd, including me of course, rushed to the exits with arms in defensive mode. Fortunately, we could all pretty much outrun him and escape the dread hug."

"Wow, Gardner might turn out to be a bit less memorable. I think he has an actual idea. Something called 'multiple intelligences.'"

"He's that guy? Oh great – I love that idea. Of course –I've heard of him. Doesn't he say there are more ways to be smart than are dreamt of in your SATs?"

"That's it," said Annette. "I remember that one of these intelligences is 'interpersonal.' The kid who works his peers like a candidate gets credit for brains. He may not know a coordinating conjunction from a cosecant, but he knows how to work a crowd."

"Well. I love that. That kid does have brains. I'd probably buy a used car from him. Alors," I said as I headed for the door, "Simon dit, 'Va à la maison.'" (Simon says, "Go home.")

"A demain." (see you tomorrow)

This particular Faculty Enrichment Day was a true lark. We arrived at the hotel to find coffee and luscious pastries laid out for our consumption. Teachers from schools all over town were milling in the lobby. Gardner's book, *Frames of Mind,* was on display and for sale. People anticipated the speech, hoping that we would learn of a more inclusive way to view students, a way which would tap into the potential of kids who usually fell through the cracks. I was also thinking that maybe there was something in this theory for Tammy.

Gardner turned out to be an engaging speaker. I had the feeling that he had that interpersonal thing nailed. He outlined his theory. First, he gave his definition of "intelligence." Among other things, he said it was the ability to solve problems. He had identified eight of these intelligences. That would be six in addition to the two that schools and tests already studied – verbal and mathematical. These six others included the interpersonal and then the intrapersonal. He cited Proust as an example of this intelligence, aptly, I thought. After all, Proust broke new ground through introspection.

When he described the bodily–kinesthetic intelligence, I had to catch my breath. He was describing Tammy. People with this intelligence understand innately their own body in space. They are dancers, athletes, and crafts people. So many images flooded my mind – Tammy dancing in the mall before she could pronounce her own name, Tammy climbing the statue and the jungle gym, Tammy fearlessly skating out onto the ice before she had received even the most rudimentary instruction, Tammy taking to the slopes, Tammy bringing home a painting and Hal saying, "Where did you get that new abstract?" and utterly incredulous when I said Tammy did it, Tammy presenting me with a flawless, beaded macramé necklace when I picked her up from camp.

The thought stayed with me as I took the subway back to Union Square. I couldn't say if Gardner advocated any particular response to strength in one of these areas. But as I mulled it, I thought that if Tammy were to get anywhere in life, if she were actually to enjoy life, it would be by spending more time doing what she was good at. People who are good at math do math and don't try to conquer their fear of trampolines. Novelists don't think they have to learn to compose a sonata. I felt elated, free from the battle to shore up her deficits. In so many ways I had failed Tammy. I had pushed her in directions where she couldn't succeed. I had felt I could manipulate her environment so that she could fire up dormant synapses and sprout new brain tendrils. I now saw I was fighting her genetic destiny. I thought that I could tease out of her DNA new paths of verbal aptitude. Had I finally seen her enough to be humbled? Let her be happy, I thought. Let her be increasingly expert in the cluster of talents that coalesced into her beautiful body in space.

Parenthood makes fools of everybody. I'd seen it a million times, parents living through their children, wishing that their kids could achieve more and better than they had. When I first got Tammy, we lived next door to a recent piano major graduate of SUNY Purchase. She was an amazing pianist whom I had watched grow up. I ran into her in the elevator, and she said she was giving lessons. I signed Tammy up.

I loved the piano. As a tiny child, I sat down in front of our parlor grand and played gorgeous cacophony with all ten fingers. My mother asked Mrs. Stroup, the organist at our church, if she would teach me. How crushed I was to discover that my first piece was nothing more than going left right left on middle C with my two thumbs.

The next piece, "Dolly Dear," caught my imagination. Though it was only two notes (CDC), I could sing it to Sally and Susan. *Dolly Dear, Go to sleep. Little stars their watch will keep.*

I hated practicing; my mother put on an egg timer every day for thirty minutes. I endured the torture. What I loved was the romance of the piano: the arpeggios, the trills, the grace notes, the lace, the fluttering chiffon.

By the time I definitely quit in the eighth grade, I could play a Chopin Waltz and stagger like a drunken sailor through Carl Philip Emanuel Bach's *Solfeggietto.*

So now I wanted Tammy to play. What I had lacked the perseverance to master, I put on this PDD-NOS child. I pushed Tammy to learn the notes and to practice, patiently weathering her storms of rage. The truth is she wasn't half bad, but she liked practicing even less than I had.

One day, shortly after Gardner's talk, Tammy flat out refused to go to her lesson. By now we had moved to the two-bedroom, and I walked over to quit on her behalf. But then I had a little epiphany. I was living through my child. If I loved the piano, then I should take the piano. By the time I got to Doreen's door, I had decided. "Doreen, how about teaching me instead of Tammy?"

The next afternoon, I picked Tammy up PS 40. "Body in space," I said to myself. "Not piano. Not anything academic." We walked down to see what kind of dance classes the Third Street Music School Settlement offered. Tammy had already taken a singing class there.

"No ballet," she said. "No pink poufy stuff."

Turns out a tap class was about to begin. This suited her fine – you got to wear a black leotard.

All year I fought it out with Chopin on the piano. Doreen started me on the famous *Nocturne 9 no 2*. The left hand nearly did me in. Meanwhile, I listened to a cassette of Claudio Arrau playing all the nocturnes. I felt a special kinship with him because he had been the teacher of Doreen's teacher. I was on a direct line to the greats. When I finally reached a place where I could move on to another piece, I told Doreen how much I loved one of the other nocturnes, 37 no 1. It sounded exquisitely airy—like an aural rendition of my grandmother's delicate tatting.

"That one's a lot easier than the one you're playing," she said. Easier and so beautiful! Good fortune was smiling. This was the first piece I ever chose for myself.

Every week, I went to Doreen; every week, Tammy went to Third Street, which by the incongruous logic of New York, was on Eleventh Street. As winter turned to spring, the annual recital was announced. Impossibly, it was on the same day as my piano recital. I scrutinized the times. Hers was in the afternoon, and mine was in the early evening, across the river in New Jersey.

The day came. Could I have been any more of a stage mother cliché, standing in front with my video camera? Out she came, tapping in a line with the rest of the shuffle stepping girls. *Brush out brush out brush out one two.* Her long hair was twisted up into a bun, and over her tights, she wore a little black circle skirt. Was it just me, or were her arms and legs longer and more graceful than anybody else's? No, I'm right. I have the videotape.

She had a moment to savor triumph and a cookie, and then the two *ar-teests* had to move on to the next event.

My recital was in a church in Hoboken. Doreen and two other teachers had combined forces. I saw with dismay that I was the last on the program. Sweaty palms for an hour, at least. They must have put us in order by age. At nearly fifty, I had no competitors. The next oldest appeared to be about seventeen. I saw that he would play *Nocturne 9 no 2*. Thank goodness I had the other nocturne. I couldn't imagine that he would play 9 worse than I did. With a different piece, at least I had a shot at not distinguishing myself as the old bad one.

Tammy sat with Doreen and her mother. The tots played the great classics from *Teaching Little Fingers How to Play*. By middle school, they trotted out *Minuet in G*. Finally, the seventeen-year-old acquitted himself nicely with the nocturne, showing skill I envied. I consoled myself with the thought that I had more dedication. He hadn't even bothered to learn the piece by heart. I felt it was a rule that you memorize the piece for a recital.

My memory held, I knew the notes, and I played with passion (some would say schmaltz). For the first time since eighth grade, I participated in a public performance. My turn to grab a little triumph and a couple of cookies.

10

SIXTH GRADE GRADUATION
AND RESPITE IN AFRICA

My father came to visit just in time for Tammy's sixth-grade graduation from PS 40 where he'd have a chance to see if he recognized anything from his days there nearly eighty years before.

Friends had already let out for the summer so I could take Tammy shopping and visit a museum or two with my dad. She wanted a new dress for the event and to my surprise went for something diaphanous and pastel.

She had neglected her beautiful hair for a long time and just pulled it back into a ponytail every day without brushing it. Abundant and fine, hers was the perfect hair to tangle and mat. When I finally tried, I couldn't get a brush through it. I took her to the beauty parlor, hoping they might have some cream to make it slimier and easier to disentangle.

Every hairdresser in the place took a crack at the mess, to the cries and shrieks of Tammy Agonistes. Whenever the door to the parlor opened, Tammy screamed, "HELP!" in hope of a rescue from the street. When she yelled at the top of her lungs, "Somebody call 911," my beautician opted for the Gordian approach and snipped out the two most offending snarls. Tammy had enough hair that the loss was imperceptible. She emerged with wavy tresses bouncing on her shoulders.

The morning of graduation, Tammy had her final vaccination. Her appointment was two hours before the ceremony. She looked so lovely in her dress, her flowing hair, and her black flats, that I figured now at age twelve, she was at last mature enough to have a shot without incident. Surely she wouldn't want to mess herself up with hysterics before the big event.

The receptionist said, "Tammy, you look very pretty."

"I'm on my way to my sixth grade graduation," Tammy replied. She smiled and tossed her hair, the picture of a budding teen.

We took a seat and Tammy began to rock in her seat. Uh-oh. Anxiety.

"I'm proud of you, Tammy," I said. "You're so grown up."

"Yup," she said.

"You can come in now," said Carlos, the mustachioed orderly. "Wow, Tammy, you're all dressed up. You going somewhere?"

"Uh-huh. Graduation."

The nurse turned to greet us as we entered the little examining room. Tammy started walking backwards.

"Whoa. This way Tammy," I said. "Let's do this so we can get to the school."

I reached for her hand. She snatched it away. "No."

Oh no, here it comes. In the few moments we had been there she was sucked back into the black hole of her early childhood. Would this never end? I felt overcome with weariness. Wait until she heard about Pap smears. She'd die of cervical cancer first.

Carlos, a gentle giant, stepped in. "Come on Tam. You're a big girl. You can do this. It will only take a second, and then you're on your way."

"No," she said and bolted for the door out of the waiting room.

Carlos caught up with her and stooped down so he could look her in the eye. "Tammy, come with me. Right now." She clutched the door jam, and screamed, "No!" "No" reverberated down the halls of Beth Israel. A tiny boy snuggled closer to his mother in alarm. So diminutive in contrast to this husky guy, she stared him down. Her firmness astonished the whole room.

How could this defiant terror be my child? I felt a strong surge of disappointment. Seven years of my nurturing and she was still unspeakably rude. Was it my job to enter the head of this little lunatic? Okay, I got it. Shots terrified her. The empathy I prided myself on was nowhere to be found. Where was the child who tried to meet expectations, to be a good girl, where did she go?

Tammy clung to the jam as the orderly scooped her up. Her body, in all its gauzy elegance, hovered parallel to the floor. Her fingers gripped the jam. She clasped it for dear life. It was the one upright tree that could withstand the hurricane. Her fright, or maybe stubbornness, made her strong.

The nurse came out to help Carlos peel her fingers from the door jam. Her body still aloft, Tammy wriggled and screamed, fighting to reestablish her grip. The nurse emerged victorious from the struggle and took Tammy's hand firmly. Tammy screamed and wept. The nurse and I exchanged glances. "The cocoon," I said.

"Tammy, why don't you sit with Mom a minute and calm down?"

"Come here, Tammy," I said. "You don't want to be late for graduation." My patience was phony. I could have killed her.

I sat down, holding her hand. I saw that she was no longer the twelve-year-old I came in with. She was three. I guessed that her inner war between her fear and all I have taught her about how you act had been lost. Fear triumphed. She yanked her hand away and before I could catch her, she backed away laughing, the taunting laugh of a tiny child playing tag. She pointed at me and stuck out her tongue.

"Tammy, this is not a game," I said.

She darted toward the hall, and ran smack into the receptionist. I caught one hand and the nurse caught the other. She was surrounded.

"Okay, Tammy," said the nurse, "this is something you have to do so you don't get sick. It's very important. Do you understand?"

Tammy looked pensive. I knew she was plotting her next escape. I chimed in, "That's right, Tammy. It's something you have to get over with. By now Poppop and Anne are waiting for us at PS 40. Let's do this, okay?" *Get with the program, you little bitch.*

She appeared calm. This tricked the nurse, but not me. Under the surface, Tammy now was fully committed to avoiding the shot. The nurse relaxed her grip, and Tammy used all her strength to jerk free of me. As she darted to the door, Carlos and another burly guy snatched her up and plunked her in the cocoon; she knew she was getting the shot. She started to sob in earnest. "You're hurting me!" she moaned.

The shot took one second.

It seemed nothing had changed except this time she was much stronger. She was too big for this. I couldn't scoop her up any more. It took two strong men to get her in the cocoon. I was disappointed in her, angry with her, tired of her. She seemed foreign. I would have been mortified to act like this even when I was five years old. Now I was mortified to be her mother. "You don like give nobody no trouble." The gypsy was right. It was true. Now I had a child who indulged her fear and gave the whole world trouble. This was what it was like to be Tammy's mother.

The butterfly emerged from the cocoon.

"Okay, Tammy, you got through it. Good for you. Let's make tracks."

It was over. Metamorphosis. *I forgive you, Tammy; I forgive you, Marge.* At least she wouldn't get typhoid or tetanus or whatever it was.

We hurried up First Avenue, a beautiful twelve-year-old and her loving mother, off to mark a milestone.

—Tammy, do you remember how you felt about shots when you were a kid?

—Hated it. I still do. They had to put me in a damn straight jacket cuz I would go nuts and I would push people and I would try to bite them.

—I forgot that.

—Oh yeah that's why they had me in a straight jacket so they could have access. They made it tight enough so they could still give me the shot.

—Remember the shot the day of your sixth grade graduation. I thought you were so big it wouldn't be a problem.

—Oh no no no. It was still a problem, I'm thirty-eight right now and it's still a problem. I have to focus on something. To block it out. I get a certain spot on the wall or whatever and I just tell her do it now. And I stay focused.

—Do you think it's a phobia?

—Don't know. Just like I don't like to mix foods. Lots of people like to mix this and this and that together, but I like it all in its own little area. I don't know why. It's just something I do, something that's a part of me. I don't know why I still haven't grown up from it.

Mr. Brynien greeted her anxiously and guided her to the line that was already going up on stage into the risers. I found Anne and my dad, who said he recognized the room, though it seemed much smaller than when he was seven.

As the video I took shows, Tammy sang her heart out. To watch her pour herself into "That's What Friends are For," you would never believe that less than an hour earlier, at least five adults were fixed on calming what to all the world looked like a crazed arachnophobe fending off a host of invading spiders. The sixth grade's grand finale was a rousingly patriotic "I'm Proud to be an American."

The principal came to offer my father a special welcome as a returning alum. He told her that he was there when the Titanic went down. She said that she knew. I'm sure Tammy told all who would listen.

At the reception in the courtyard, Tammy and her classmates signed yearbooks. We had bought a quarter page ad thanking Mr. Brynien for three great years. Tammy would be going across the street to JHS 104 in the fall. I had my fingers crossed.

In the meantime, Tammy, my father, and I all headed in different directions for summer break. The Wall had come down long since and now East Germany had merged into Germany. My father had always dreamed of visiting Luther country, but for all the years of the Cold War, he was discouraged from visiting East Germany.. At eighty-six, he saw his opportunity. After visiting us, he went to New Jersey to join my brother and nephew for one more trip to Europe. I could imagine how Wittenberg, the city of Luther, would rejuvenate him, especially the door of Castle Church, for him the sacred portal where, tradition has it, Luther nailed the Ninety-five Theses.

Tammy went to Camp Huntington again, and this time, I took a TAP Air Portugal flight first to Lisbon and then to Abidjan, Ivory Coast.

Respite, adventure, cultural exchange, and propaganda for *la belle langue*, all rolled into one. As soon as people knew I was making this trip, they gave me contacts, and I was invited to stay in the home of an embassy worker for two nights and then with a family. The mother was an American who had met her Ivoirian husband when she was in the Peace Corps. The couple worked to improve health care by promoting the use of condoms both for birth control and AIDS prevention. I sat in on a meeting where I learned that most prenatal care was limited to the hours after labor had begun.

Equipped with gifts of notebooks, pencils, and pens, I visited an orphanage just outside of Abidjan. The appreciative personnel told me that there was an infirmary, but that it had no Band-Aids, no painkiller, and no quinine, so important for the treatment of malaria. I spent the afternoon answering questions from these children who wanted to know everything about their American counterparts. Their big query was "are they any good at soccer?"

Everywhere I went, children surrounded me begging for "des bics, des bics, Madame, s'il vous plaît." I guess they learned that American women usually had at least one ballpoint pen in their purses. I brought a few hundred.

I climbed aboard a bus that bounced its way along the unpaved red clay roads to the coastal town of Sassandra. The VCR in the front played Chinese martial arts movies dubbed in French to the delight of the young men crowded into the seats and aisles. Bumping through the barren Ivoirian countryside, punctuated occasionally by a termite condominium, was this continental nexus on wheels: Africans watching Asians speak a European language in the company of an American. Wherever the bus stopped, women wrapped in colorful pagnes, emerged with huge tray-like hats, laden with snacks, candies and tobacco products for sale, all balanced deftly on their heads,

I stayed in a little room under a mosquito net. Outside my door was a "maquis," an outdoor restaurant. Many men approached my table as I ate, begging me to take them back to the States, offering to be my servant. On the last day, the wife of the owner of the maquis, a blue and gold printed pagne wrapped around her head in a turban, came up to my table. Her husband was away and her three tiny children clung to *maman*.

"Pardon, Madame. Do you work?" she asked timidly in beautiful, cultivated French.

"Yes."

"Where's your husband?"

"I don't have a husband. "

"No husband?"

"No."

"You work and keep your money?"

"Yes."

"Oh, very nice," she said, her eyes suddenly brimming with tears.

Until this moment, I had assumed that she was happy, that she knew nothing of greater independence and gender equality. Now I felt the sorrow of her narrowly proscribed life. Now I saw her suppressed longing for something better. I had listened to all the stories of sad men who wanted to come to America to be my servant, knowing that I could not possibly give them the least hope. I had been on the defensive. "I'm a teacher," I told them. "I don't have servants." My mere presence there was proof to them that I had unimaginable wealth. This time I really wished I had the resources. If I had wanted marriage and a family, it certainly wasn't like this. I think I would have gone mad if I had had to wait until my husband went away to sneak a furtive conversation with another human being.

When I picked Tammy up at camp, a counselor came running to warn me that Tammy had had a little diving mishap. Her fake diamond stud was embedded in her earlobe. Otherwise, she explained as we drove back to the city, she had a fine time.

"Did you make any new friends?"

"I hung out with Mike Gibson."

"That's funny. My friend Jan Gibson has a son named Mike, but it can't be the same one," I said.

"Does he drool?" she said.

Definitely a different one.

I took her to Beth Israel. They assured me that over time the earring would work its way through without medical intervention. A cubic zirconium stud would pass entirely through her earlobe. I was home.

PART III
1991-1998

11

JUNIOR HIGH – NOT GREAT

At Friends, I generally taught the fifth and sixth grade French students, the seniors in Advanced Placement French, and a couple of levels in between. Among the fifth graders I always had a little coterie that loved me. I recommend fifth graders for adults with self-esteem issues. Ten-year-olds can't wait to tell you about all the joys and sorrows of their lives from hamster deaths to grandma's postcards from Paris.

But by seventh grade, my little best friends no longer knew me. They didn't greet me in the hall. If I greeted them, they looked put upon and startled. They had eyes only for their friends. A developmental and behavioral pediatrician came to talk to us one Faculty Enrichment Day, and he explained that the teacher's goals for a class diverge sharply from the goals of our seventh and eighth graders. I, for instance, wanted to impart the mechanics of negative expressions or the crazy way the French place their object pronouns before the verb. The kids wanted to avoid being humiliated in front of their peers or to score some points by making the teacher look stupid. No wonder middle schoolers are worse at pronunciation. The younger ones think it's fun to poke their lips forward and say the French "U" sound. Seventh graders would rather die than look weird.

So I am familiar with the phenomenon of adult loss of influence with the twelve and thirteen-year-old. I expected trouble. What I didn't expect was that Tammy's education would come to a screeching halt and that for the eight years she continued to go to school after her graduation from the sixth grade, she would never again experience school as a place for excitement about learning.

One day I came home early and found Tammy watching TV.

"Why aren't you in school?"

"I'm expelled."

"No. You can't be expelled. They would have to call me first."

"I think they tried to."

"What on earth did you do?"

"Nothing! It wasn't my fault. I never even go to the cafeteria. I buy pizza on First Avenue. I just went there once last week to talk to Anthony and somebody shouts, 'Food fight' and I mean bagels are flying through the air, you know those little ketchup packets, I got hit by one of those and spaghetti with sauce, it was disgusting. Everything's flying. You name it. So then the teachers get all mad and I get blamed. Nothing happened to Anthony."

"Did you say 'last week'? How long have you been out of school?"

"About a week."

"Oy vey ist mir. You have been walking to First Avenue with me every day and then doubling back?"

"Uh-huh. Hey, what are you doing?"

"Calling 104, what do you think?"

I reached the vice principal, Mr. Sachs.

"No, I don't know about a food fight. I see Tammy has been absent for two weeks."

"Oh my God. And nobody called me? I had no idea that she was out of school. For the record, I expect her to attend regularly and if she's sick, I'll call."

My fury was evenly divided between the school and Tammy. What was wrong with that school? She could have dropped off the face of the earth and no one would have cared. How could they be so nonchalant about a student missing two weeks? Was I the only parent who gave a damn about their child?

She could be another Lisa Steinberg for all they knew. Remember her? Her illegal father Joel Steinberg killed her, and the PS 41 staff had failed to note red flags.

And what was with that child? She should have been a fiction writer. She embroidered that whopper in two seconds flat. Food fight my eye!

Did she have the slightest notion of the difference between true and false? Surely she knew I would find out there was no food fight.

But she never reported accurately. I could believe nothing of what she said. Her reality was only tangential at best to what happened. Every day she starred as heroine or victim in some sitcom version of events. The food fight story was normal by comparison with her usual stream of lies; I mean it was normal to lie to get out of an infraction like skipping school day after day. Usually she lied for no apparent reason.

What infuriated me was the smoothness of two weeks' worth of deception. I hadn't suspected a thing. Every day at supper she had related her adventures at school when she had actually been sitting in her bedroom with her feet up watching Jerry Springer.

"There was no food fight. Mr. Sachs never heard of any food fight. You are not expelled. Why aren't you going to school?"

"Felix is going to kill me if I don't give him $40."

"Jeez. Tammy, would you just spit out the truth?"

Bearing in mind my source, I would never know the truth, the whole truth and nothing but the truth. The best I could make out from her was that a classmate named Felix claimed he loaned her $40. Now he wanted it back. Tammy swore ("I swear to God") that she never borrowed any money from him.

I sat down, breathed deeply, and tried to understand. Maybe the lunch money I gave Tammy was a little more than what others got. Maybe she had bought a slice or two for other kids, enjoyed the rush of the friendship she purchased, and created the impression that there was more where that came from. Maybe the nothing we had was more than the nothing they had. Feeling she was in the wrong, she adjusted her memories to exculpate or aggrandize herself. Yet Tammy almost never reported accurately and the more detailed her account, the farther it was from what actually happened. Tammy had found an additional reason to lie: entertainment.

Was this her disability? What was this? We all lie or fudge a little when we are in the wrong. We all see reality through our own lens. Recounting what happened is not like science, which requires replication to establish truth. We see it once as a gestalt and then pull up details until we have what we think is a full picture. But who is to say which of those details is constructed from whole cloth and which we teased directly out of our hippocampus?

In remembering an event there are those whose recall is close to a video, and, at the other end, there must be others who make it all up. Maybe Tammy is just one of those at this end of the spectrum. Her troubled history had massively distorted her lens. When it came to seeing reality, she could probably be declared legally blind.

Oh, shut up, Marge. Lord, I even annoy myself, I'm such a casuist. The kid was bad. Ground her. Is it really necessary to devise a treatise on Truth?

"Tammy, we call this extortion. Felix is trying to extort money from you. No way this is happening."

I made an appointment with the Mr. Sachs, who turned out to be a large enough guy to command adolescent respect. Felix, a very cute kid who undoubtedly could wield power in the Special Ed set, was in the room. I was not allowed to address him directly. He stuck to his story that Tammy had borrowed $40 from him.

"Okay," I said, "if Felix loaned her the money, he must have gotten it from his mother, unless he has a job."

The vice principal asked and Felix said that he didn't have a job. Tammy had intimated that he sold drugs, but it was unlikely he'd mention that in this office. Then again, also, likely not true.

I said that in that case, I'd write a check to his mother, and that would be the end of it. He was not to loan Tammy any more money. Felix didn't look happy. Two weeks later the school called to tell me the mother had returned my check. She had never given Felix anything like $40 dollars.

The energy at 104 went into these peer conflicts, at least in the Special Ed part. The school constantly negotiated he said/she said soap operas that were far removed from the great disciplines of language arts, history, science, and math. What excited the imagination of the students was conflict, betrayal, love, infidelity, and secrets. Learning wasn't on their radar and the adults were too indifferent, preoccupied, or burnt out to ignite new fires of curiosity. Tammy, with her talent for spinning out fictions, filled the void.

—What happened with Felix?

—Him and his stupid little cousin tried to get me to pay for everything for them. For their lunches, give them money whenever they wanted.

—Who was his cousin?

—Eric Figueroa.

—Oh yeah. There was this whole thing when you thought you couldn't go to school because you thought he would kill you.

—Yeah, because when I tried to fight back he would threaten me.

—Do you remember how it was resolved?

—We had a conference—you and Mr. Sachs and him, and you wrote a check to his parents, which they tried to give back because of the fact that they didn't even know. Then his second cousin from Puerto Rico, Yolanda, (she said this with her best Spanish accent) came and oh my God I wanted to kill that girl cause she said I heard you talking bad about my cuz. So I said your cuz is a person who tries to escort money off people instead of asking his own parents.

—Didn't he become friends with you later?

—Yeah, but I never really trusted his friendship – because how would I know when he would try to get money from me. It was a friendship that wasn't very trustworthy.

—Tam, did you learn anything at 104?

—What do you mean?

—School stuff.

—Not much.

I take it back (somewhat) that Tammy never again experienced the joy of learning in school. The clarinet was one bright spot. Mr. Keane was a fine musician, and for band Tammy was mainstreamed, so for that class she was with the regular population of the school. In New York, Special Education had grown to be one of three separate but unequal systems. People who could afford to send their child to private school got to know the ins and outs of the arcane admissions procedures of independent schools. Sometimes in my travels I would meet someone who grew up in Manhattan, I would ask where they went to school, and they would say Dalton, or Trinity, or the UN School or Little Red or any one of the other elite enclaves that dotted the island. When I said I taught at Friends, they would play "Do You Know" with me and it would always turn out that we knew someone in common. I was part of a small town superimposed on a giant city.

In the larger world of public education there was Regular Ed of about a million kids and Special Ed, which had about forty thousand. The Regular Ed kids subdivided further in high school when many of the more able students were syphoned off into schools like Stuyvesant High, LaGuardia, and Bronx Science, which required a test or audition for admittance. Tammy lived in the domain of Special Ed except for music.

She took to the instrument. I asked Mr. Keane if he knew of anyone who could give her private lessons. He said that he could. Every week he came to our house and pushed her to play *String of Pearls* and *Cotton-Eye Joe*. One day he told us that there were going to be auditions for the Borough-Wide Band. He thought Tammy had a shot and when the concert came, it would be at Carnegie Hall.

Rehearsals were every Saturday morning, so of course Tammy wanted no part of it.

"Tammy, this is a chance to play at Carnegie Hall!"

"So?"

The term "Tiger Mom" was not in vogue in that era, but I recognize that I was one. All her life she would be able to say that she played at Carnegie Hall. Professional musicians would give their right arm for those bragging rights. I rolled over her objections.

"You're going. Let's go."

"I hate you!"

"I don't care. You're doing this."

She passed the audition and was in the third clarinet section. Any kid in Manhattan who wanted to could try out. Most were from Regular Ed with a few from the private schools. We saw no other kids from her cohort.

Every Saturday the same struggle played out. She didn't want to get up. She didn't want to go. I was having none of it. Eventually the sullen adolescent stomped out of her bedroom and said, "Okay, okay." Her scowl was so intense that it occurred to me to say, "Gee Tammy, someone could tap dance on your lower lip," but I restrained myself. I kept my eye on the goal.

Half way through the year, things eased up. Tammy would tell my friends that she was going to play at Carnegie Hall. Their reaction led her to wonder if perhaps this might be a cool thing after all.

At last the concert came. For once I was seated in the orchestra, a perk of being the mother of a performer. Usually I was in the nosebleed section, but for this concert, everyone was in the orchestra. The balconies were dark. All the attendees were parents and siblings of the musicians.

In addition to the band, there was a citywide chorus and a citywide orchestra. Normally the Carnegie Hall orchestra section was booked by the crème de la crème. This time its denizens were, like me, the lait du lait. Many of the parents had apparently never been to a concert before. If their child was not in the group performing at that moment, they felt it was proper to roam the aisles munching Fritos. Still, they were there. The membrane that enclosed the world of classical music had been breached. The Big Apple invited the have-nots into the inner sanctum.

The concert, imperfect in its execution of course – these were kids after all –was a marvel of intersecting forces, from the city with wisdom enough to encourage the effort of students and teachers to the audience, who, through their love of their own children, perhaps felt a power of music they had never known before. Like the Metropolitan Museum for Sroeun, the Borough-Wide City-Wide Concert provided transcendent moments when income limitation fell away and the portals to the sublime achievements of the human imagination opened wide.

I wept through the entire performance. There is nothing more touching than young people doing their best. And when the children are the rich mix of races and ethnicities of the city of New York, all giving up their Saturday mornings of sleeping in to join together to encounter Beethoven and Copland, then I'm verklempt.

Tammy did it. I was so proud. I bought her a flower, and when I collected her at the stage door, I saw a look of flushed triumph that meant it was worth it; she was proud of herself. "I played at Carnegie Hall!"

"You did."

"Wow."

12
EDUCATIONAL CHAOS

Tammy now had her own keys and could come home from school on her own. Often after school we would take our bikes over to the East River and pedal down to the Williamsburg Bridge. If we felt like it, we would go all the way to the Brooklyn Bridge or the South Street Seaport.

Tammy took figure skating lessons at Sky Rink, on the top floor of a building on the west side of Midtown Manhattan. In the summer, when we were being stewed alive in our apartment, she would take off to skate. "Don't forget your gloves," I would remind her as the mercury rose up into the 90's. Both of us recognized the hard to fathom fact that shortly she would need them. She took the bus by herself to Eighth Avenue.

Tammy was beginning to have a life apart from me. One day I came home early when I was supposed to stay late for a faculty meeting. As I came through the door exhausted and ready to lie down for a nap, I found Tammy entertaining her friend Mercedes, an exotic beauty of Ecuadorian descent, who resembled a young Sophia Loren, and a very deferential boy named Anthony, from Harlem. Mercedes had been in Mr. Brynien's class but had gone to Junior High School a year before Tammy. She was speech impaired, which in such a pretty girl only added to her mysterious charm. They were listening to music in the living room and Anthony, particularly, greeted me politely. The sweet cloying smell of cheap perfume or eau de toilette filled the air. I went to my bedroom wondering why my home smelled like a Turkish brothel. As soon as I lay down, I knew. Under the sweetness was the unmistakable smell of cigarettes. Lucky for Tammy, I was too tired to let them have it.

Another time I came home to find the chain lock up on my door.

"Let me in, Tammy!"

"Just a minute."

I could hear a flurry of activity and whispers of dismay. At last a bare-footed Anthony took down the chain and let me in. He said he had to get going as he pulled on his shoes and socks. Amazing. A year earlier I had been worrying about her imperfectly completed toilet training. Now she was locking herself in the apartment with a boy, the first of what I came to think of as her own personal rainbow coalition. It wasn't surprising that she had chosen a black boy. Tammy just didn't notice any difference, or rather she noticed it, but it was as unimportant as eye color.

Anthony was her boyfriend through the years at 104. He took the bus down from Harlem, where he lived with his grandmother, every day. His mother was in and out of his life. Anthony tolerated Tammy's sullen moods at least as well as I did. When I gave in to Tammy too easily, he said, "You don't have to do what she says, you know"—helpful parenting advice from a boy whose grandmother had taught him respect. Anthony was a Jehovah Witness and spoke with warmth of the many adults guiding him at Kingdom Hall. He was a MIS 1 kid like Tammy, but he was determined to compensate for his learning issues with hard work. I don't know what placed him in Special Ed. He said that school was hard for him, but if he really put his mind to it, he could do anything.

Anthony, Tammy, and I would go downstairs and sit on a bench and talk. He said that his neighborhood was really scary. Even if they had no milk, his grandmother would not let him out after 8 o'clock, not that he wanted to go. He could hear the occasional pop of a gun and was happy to be inside. He was into capoeira, a Brazilian martial art that looked to me more like dance. He began with the jinga. It looked like graceful acrobatics: he would take large strides back and forth and end up doing a cartwheel. Before long, Tammy was into it with him.

—Tammy, do you know what iambic pentameter is?

—Iambic pen whaaaa?

—Iambic pentameter.

—God bless you!

When she graduated from 104, Tammy went into the tenth grade at Murry Bergtraum, a large public high school right by the Brooklyn Bridge. I was worried. With the college-bound kids syphoned off into the private schools and competitive high schools, I feared that the message that Tammy and company were not meant to love education would be further reinforced.

We went together to an evening of meet and greet with the teachers. Her English teacher, an affable young Chinese man, said, "Tommy, good student."

I could forgive him calling her Tommy, but a sentence with no verb? This was her ENGLISH teacher. Still, I liked the "good student" part, and she didn't complain at first.

Maybe this was because she met a tall handsome Chinese boy named Jack. He lived in Chinatown and spoke Chinese, Cantonese I suppose, at home. He struggled to communicate in English, smiled often, and conveyed the good manners of a strict upbringing.

Tammy had been there a month or so when I got a call, a summons really, to come in for a parent conference. When I showed up, I found myself in the hot seat. An entire committee was seated in a circle, looking at me. As Tammy often says, "Uh-oh, what did I do?"

The chair of the group explained that Tammy had been "making out" with Jack at the back of their history class. I laughed. This was the federal case I was brought in for? Why didn't the teacher just tell them to stop? Finding that I alone was amused, I quickly sobered up. They apparently expected me to answer for her.

"Do you think this is a good way to behave?

"No. No, I don't." Who did they think I was? Oh sure, at Friends Seminary we insist that students couple up in snuggle mode before we teach them.

"Do you think this is the way other young people behave?"

I couldn't restrain myself. "Well, Jack behaved this way." I got a titter from one of the ladies. I also observed that Jack's mother wasn't there.

I said I would talk with Tammy and that I sincerely hoped she would not be a repeat offender. Lucky me. This time I got off with only a slap on the wrist.

Tammy blew off our little talk, but Jack was never heard from again. Maybe they did call in his mother.

Immediately a Hispanic boy named William appeared in our home.

So boys, one after the other. The black boy, then the Chinese boy, and now the Puerto Rican boy.

I thought I was self-effacing enough before I got her. But raising her provided daily lessons in humility. At first I thought this little girl is a tabula rasa on which I will inscribe everything good, true and beautiful. Or she was a bone-dry vessel into which I would pour great potions. But she was formed and filled already. Though she was raised away from her four brothers, she was always more comfortable with boys. Thomas and Michael were her great pals at Friends Seminary, and all the way through PS 40 she spent weekends playing with her brothers Matt and Martin. She liked to run, climb, and jump. So boys. She gravitated to boys. She led the way with her brothers and gave them what-for. She didn't try to please them. She competed with them, palled around with them, led them by the nose.

I envied her. One of us was screwed up, but which one was it? To me, men were inscrutable and other. Even superior. If they weren't better than I, their maleness was in question. I got that from my mother. When she met my father, she thought he was smart and good-looking, but maybe too faint-hearted. She challenged him to a race to the end of the road. In her mind, she determined to have nothing further to do with him if he couldn't win. He must have known what was at stake and beat her for the first and last time. I grew up like Simone de Beauvoir, imbued with the idea that men are the icheban of the genders. If objectively a guy was dumber or more dull-witted than this humble member of the second sex, what good was he?

My best friend in grade school, Masha, wanted to be a boy. "Come on," she said, "it's better to be a boy. They get to do everything."

But I thought they got to do everything because they were genuinely entitled. And I didn't mind because I would get to be a mother. I went around singing, "I Enjoy Being a Girl," like some demented musical comedy ingénue, feeling that the boy for me would have to be smarter than I was, funnier, more energetic, more ambitious – especially more ambitious. He would be the sun and I would be the moon, basking in reflected light. I bought it all. My brain couldn't break through the construct of conventionality and see the opposite sex as just people. I was in my twenties with the new wave of feminism crashing onto my shore before I had an inkling of what Tammy knew all along.

Her taste in boys, however, was not infallible. This new boy, William, was delusional and claimed connection with highly placed entertainers and law enforcement personnel. "If anything happens with Tammy, I'll take care of it. I know people." He said he would introduce Tammy to his friend Mariah Carey. He seemed to think that bourgeois Stuyvesant Town was "the projects," and advised me to get her out of there. Apparently, I could do as his mother had and find a run-down brownstone in Brooklyn.

By November, Tammy was begging to get out of this school, and she had plenty of ammunition. "I'm not learning anything." "I don't like being there at all." "I have to get out of this school." "There are gangs and I don't feel safe." "This girl with her two friends, she comes at me with her little posse—and she got all in my face, and I was in the center going 'What did I do?'" I spoke with Gerry and we agreed that this school wasn't working out for Tammy.

My friend Diana, from church, was a social worker who had taught English in Japan. She was out of work, so I hired her for the three weeks in December before the Christmas break, hoping I could figure something out by that time. In our living room, she gave Tammy lessons in Japanese culture—dance and calligraphy and science. They studied the great earthquake disasters in Japan. Diana figured out how to make tectonic plates in a bucket of sand and then to simulate an earthquake. On the last day, Diana and Tammy donned kimonos, performed a tea ceremony for me, and then sang a Japanese song while dancing and waving fake cherry blossoms. It was like the good old days of Mr. Brynien.

Japan from all angles. This was the kind of education I loved: integrated—science, history, language, art, culture, geography. Tammy had been happy and involved every minute.

When I evaluated other teachers as part of my job, my first and perhaps only criterion was involvement. Were the kids actively engaged in learning? I saw an English class where the teacher, a poet herself, asked the kids for examples of eighth grade survival tips. "Don't wear the same shirt twice in a row." "Don't tell your mom everything." The advice accumulated. Then the teacher helped the class to arrange this collective wisdom into iambic pentameter. "Wear not the shirt worn yesterday again." "With mom (though nice) your secrets are not safe." The students were empowered. They were poets; they were wise. I wanted Tammy to be excited about iambic pentameter.

Education wasn't much if it didn't light up the imagination. Trends in foreign language teaching had changed over the years, and I liked the direction they were going. The most recent texts advised students to imagine they were with French friends. Ask your French friends what they do on the weekend or ask them what they generally eat for lunch. I believe that the students who truly imagined French friends were more successful at learning. They thought, "Oh, I want to talk with them. How do I say this? How do I get this so they'll understand me?"

Tammy loved learning with Diana as she had with Mr. Brynien. I felt defeated. Why couldn't I find a school that would fire her up again?

We visited a small private school in mid-town called The Tutoring School. They worked one-on-one with students. Tammy and I liked it, and I signed her up right away. I figured I had enough savings to cover a month or two while I figured something out with the Board of Ed.

Mercedes was going to a private school in Queens at no expense to her family. I called her mother. She gave me the name of a lawyer but said that I would have to do the fighting. For $350, the lawyer taught me to say, "This school does not meet my daughter's needs." It was money well spent. It's the law that a school must meet a child's needs.

I was working on two fronts. I was trying to find a school for the next year, and I was requesting a teacher for her for the rest of this school year. My argument was that since Murry Bergtraum did not meet her needs, the Board of Ed needed to furnish her some alternate form of education. They gave me a list of special needs schools in the area. In the first, I saw a large child count to two and receive thrilled applause from the staff. Tammy was doing algebra. "This school does not meet my daughter's needs."

I went to another school along the East River. They were very welcoming and let me visit an eighth-grade class. The teacher asked a girl to let me look at her notebook. In it, there was a test. One question caught my eye. "What is the function of the penis?" The girl had answered, "To deliver urine and semen." She got a third off for this answer. The teacher's note said, "You forgot pleasure." I liked this school, I even liked their insistence that girls know the three most important aspects of the male member, but it only went up to the ninth grade. "This school does not meet my daughter's needs."

The Tutoring School called to tell me that William was hanging around and keeping Tammy from learning. I was relieved when the school system came through with a teacher for Tammy. He reminded me of Irving's description of Ichabod Crane so much that now when I try to remember his name I can only come up with "Ichabod." Normally, he went to visit kids who were hospitalized to keep them from falling behind with their class. In this case, he would meet Tammy in the Hamilton Fish Library on the lower east side and teach her all her subjects.

"Are you learning anything, Tammy?"

"Mostly he just says, 'Here, read this.'"

"Okay."

"Then he gets mad because Anthony and Mercedes are waiting for me."

"Sounds great."

Through all this, she continued with figure skating, and now I found a course in calligraphy for her at a Japanese center. She was the only Caucasian. The other students were there because their Japanese parents wanted their second-generation children to have a sense of their culture, which they were only too pleased to share with us. Tammy loved the ritual. They each greeted the teacher, "Ohayou gozaimasu, sensei," and bowed.

In a moment of enthusiasm, I signed us up for a sign language course at our church. Tammy caught on much better than any of the rest of us. It was really a case of Tammy and the rest of the class. When the teacher asked me the word for Tuesday, I saw Tammy bury her head in her hands. Instead of Tuesday, I had said, "Fuck you." She was the only member of the class who knew until the teacher graciously wrote the words on the board with a big question mark.

Tammy turned sixteen in February. William disappeared and Anthony was ready to resume his rightful place. I hired a limo, sat in the front with the driver, and let the kids enjoy the lap of luxury on the way to Sky Rink. They skated for an hour then came down to take a royal tour of the tip of Manhattan. I could hear Tammy and Mercedes razzing Anthony for the spills he took on the ice.

13
HALLOWEEN

Raising Tammy was its own assertiveness training course. I called the Board of Education in the spring and asked what kind of placement was left for my MIS 1(Modified Instructional Services one, i.e, Special Ed first level) girl. I had visited every school they gave me and none met her needs, to say the least.

"Oh," said the tired voice, "I don't see anything at the moment."

"WHAT??? Are you telling me that my daughter will have no education for two years in a row? I've put up with this all year, this no school that meets her needs. We can't have another year of this. She doesn't get to be sixteen again. I've visited every school you've given me. They were for people who can't count to two. My daughter does algebra and passed her RCT in math!" Most of Fourteenth Street must have heard this little outburst.

"Well, Ms. Gonzalez . . ."

"Dr. Gonzalez."

"Well, Dr. Gonzalez, there is one opening at the Lowell School."

"We'll take it." That was Mercedes' school. What had taken them so long? Now there was just one iffy place left. The system that serves a million plus students MIGHT have a place for Tammy. Merci beaucoup.

"Well, it's a private school, so you will have to meet the admissions director, and you'd better hurry because there is just that one place."

"Give me the number."

The admissions director, Ms. Grant, said she could see us at 10:00. Could I get there?

"Sure." I looked at my watch. It was after 9:00.

I was completely unfamiliar with Queens; Manhattan people rarely venture into the outer boroughs. My sister-in-law's Toyota had passed down the food chain to my niece, Becky, and then to me. So I had a car. Ms. Grant gave me directions to take the BQE, then the Grand Central then turn then turn. Pray.

Tammy was sleeping.

"Get up. We're going to the Lowell School."

I pulled her perfect little black dress out of the closet and threw it to her.

"Get cracking. We have to be there by ten. With any luck you'll be going to school with Mercedes next year."

She was pulling the dress over her head as we walked out the door. We were on the Grand Central parkway when our lane suddenly became Exit Only in heavy traffic. Now we were going toward JFK on the Van Wyck. I fumed my way to the next cloverleaf that seemed to double back. *Please Lord.*

No one is an atheist in combat or when lost in Queens.

The school was a small building tucked behind the main street into a little triangle. Ms. Grant, teased red hair and overbearing charm, greeted us. Tammy looked like a perfect angel. She got in. She would have to repeat the tenth grade.

At first she took a school bus, but she complained bitterly about the driver, who, she said, berated the students and smoked constantly. I paid her no mind until I watched the driver purposely speed off to avoid picking up a child who had run all the way from her last stop. Tammy got her way. Public transportation. She had to get to Grand Central Station, take the 7 train to Main Street Flushing and then take another bus.

Halloween was our favorite holiday. Once when Tammy was little, I draped some white window sheers around her and handed her a bouquet of plastic roses. She was a beautiful bride. When she called "Trick or treat" at the apartment of two bachelors, one young guy exclaimed, "That's the scariest costume I've seen!" Now she was too old to go begging, so we opted to have a costume party

I wrote the words and Tammy designed the spooky invitation. *Teens and their Parents Invited. How scary is that?* The invited and the uninvited showed up in droves. Tammy had carved an intricate jack-o-lantern and I devised a menu of entirely black and orange food. The buffet consisted of black bean chili on orange rice, carrots and black olives and cantaloupe with deep purple grapes. The punch was orange soda with vanilla ice cream ghosties floating in it.

Tammy was a Spanish senorita in a flouncy black and red Flamenco dress, covered with sequins. Or as she would say, "A dress with sequels." In her hair, she wore a red rose, and she carried a lacy black fan to flip open when her words required dramatic effect.

I sat down next to the mother of a young man with about a dozen safety pins embedded in his right earlobe.

"Watch out for Susie over there," she told me as she lit up the first ever cigarette to be smoked in my house with my permission. "His first time out and my son caught the clap. Can you believe it? First time out!"

Tammy's beau for the evening was Joey, a boy she had met in summer camp. Things had not been going well between them, and I saw him sidling up to Mercedes, a Cowboy's cheerleader and pompom girl for the event. Then I saw Tammy making headway with a boy who had come with her schoolmate, Carol. I gave him a good look. I thought this boy, Floyd, was the most beautiful boy I had ever seen. "Tammy," I said, "didn't he come with Carol?"

"Don't worry. They're just friends. They live in the same group home."

"Okay," I said.

The first lesson I learned in the parenting course I took at that first agency before I even knew about Tammy was "don't interfere in the kids' business unless it violates your own rules." I should have had it engraved somewhere right up with "this school does not meet my child's needs."

Tammy had made her room into a ghost house. She filched a few grapes to peel for the eyeballs everyone would have to touch. And scream, of course. She got Mercedes to help her guide the guests through the Cavern of the Dead. They must have had some wet spaghetti intestines in there too.

I was draped with beads and wrapped in an embroidered shawl, with a silk scarf tied around my head. I staked out a little booth to read palms. "Madame Claire Voyante sees all knows all. Discover your fate. . . . if you dare."

The line formed. They all wanted to know their futures. I made it a point to always find a long lifeline and a well-defined intersecting love line. Give the customers what they want. One mom seemed particularly relieved but wanted an extra consultation about her sister. I saw that she sincerely thought I had some telepathic power. I told her I would really have to see her sister's palm.

But I didn't have the gift. I could not guess when I looked at Floyd's palm that a few years down the road he would be the father of my only grandchild, and that if palms meant anything, he would surely have a deep but brief love line with Tammy's name written on it.

14
NOBODY'S PERFECT

After a rapid succession of boyfriends, Tammy settled on Scott, a developmentally disabled, cheerful inhabitant of the same group home as Carol and Floyd. Scott came with us to the Community Church, proudly became a member, and found a mentor among the parishioners. He glommed onto us and occupied Tammy's after school hours. Once when she fell into her non-communicative, pouty, stomping pit, he took it upon himself to call 911. He didn't know what else to do, but calling her mom could possibly have been a better idea, especially since he and Tammy were right outside our building. The ambulance arrived, the paramedics caught her, she resisted, they put her into a straight jacket, and prepared to take her to St. Vincent's ER. A paramedic called me from downstairs and let me ride with her to the hospital. Scott wanted to go too, but I figured he'd helped enough. This was the kind of thing I dealt with routinely. A sashimi deluxe would have done the trick. Now I would have to spend the night in the hospital.

They gave her a shot of something that worked as well as raw fish, but certainly not better.

The attending decided not to admit her and let me take her home. Now sane, she contended that Scott was just a jerk.

A few days later, the agency in charge of Scott's care asked me to come in for a talk. At the office in Queens, social workers, caregivers from the group home, and Scott were seated at the table. They asked why Tammy could not raise her child in our home. I came prepared to defend my decision not to let him ride in the ambulance. This was a whole new wrinkle. What were they talking about?

"What child?" I said.

They explained. Tammy had apparently told the boy that she had a small child, a daughter, who had been forcibly removed from her custody, and she wanted her child back. It was a matter of justice. Scott wanted to help her, and half the school got involved in the project of returning Tammy's child to her.

"She doesn't have a child," I sighed. Everyone appeared astonished.

"Tammy and I live in a small apartment. I think I would have noticed a baby."

"Scott," said a social worker triumphantly, "there is no child. Tammy made it up."

All eyes turned to Scott.

I understood that the adults in his life wanted him out of Tammy's clutches. I wasn't too crazy about this relationship myself. We all felt Tammy's big fat PDD-NOS or PTSD lie or soap opera lie would surely toll the death knell for this relationship.

"She lied to you, Scott."

Scott tried to take it in. There was no little girl for him to help Tammy raise. Everything had changed in a second. He took a long moment to decide what to do.

Never underestimate the power of young love. At last, with a philosophical head waggle, he said, "Nobody's perfect."

My father now lived in an independent living apartment in a high rise along the Caloosahatchee River, in Fort Myers. I loved his view of twin bridges. I got a call that he was ailing. Tammy and I got plane tickets for the weekend. We enlisted Scott to take care of Tinacat. Mushy Mushy had finally expired at the age of twenty. We found my father on the second floor, a hospital-like facility for residents who had been pushed out of the hospital before they were able to resume normal life. Two speech pathologists told me that food was going into his lungs when he ate. They said they had seen that all textures went down the wrong tube. This would kill him. I saw the pictures and okayed a feeding tube. My father loved food. There seemed little hope that he would eat anything by mouth ever again.

They also told me that there were no places available in their assisted living section and that I needed to take him to New York. There was no time for pondering a decision. I saw that it was necessary. He had to come home with me. An ambulance took him to the airport and another picked him up at LaGuardia. We got home late only to find Scott in our apartment waiting for Tammy. I kicked him out, no small feat, gave my bed to my father, and opened up a futon for myself. Exhausted, I became aware that I was glad he would spend his last days with us, his family, rather than in a lonely facility.

Tammy began to find Scott annoying, though she still wore his trendy leather jacket, and he still showed up at church. Her new friend was named Auric. Both Tammy and Auric were trying to get regular high school diplomas. Most of their classmates would get IEP (Individualized Education Plan) diplomas, which represent effort and attendance. But to get a regular diploma at that time, Tammy and Auric would have to pass Regents Competency Tests in all the major disciplines. Tammy passed the math exam at 104. She passed a few more. But she failed the history exam. The question was an essay comparing and contrasting Hitler and Mandela. She said they had both done a lot for their country.

"You know, Tammy, they might want you to mention which one was bad and which one was good."

"Hitler was bad, right?"

Auric came home with Tammy every day. Usually he ate with us. He claimed not to like humans.

"Well, Auric, I hate to break this to you, but you're a human yourself."

"Oh, no, I'm not."

"Then what are you?" I asked.

"An elf."

I loved this quirky kid. He advised me on my first computer purchase. He showed me how to use it. He called his backpack "the kitchen sink." For a couple of years he was a member of the family. Sometimes he said he was depressed.

"Why?" I asked.

"The kitchen sink weighs more than I do."

One day when I was still at work, Tammy came home with Auric and a friend, Michael. They found my father stranded in the tub. He had fallen in as he tied his shoes and was too weak to get out. He cried for help all day. The nurse who was supposed to come in the morning rang from downstairs and got my answering machine. It said, of course, that I was away. So she figured my father was away.

Michael, a strapping lad, picked my father up and put him on the bed while Auric called 911. Then Tammy called the school and had the secretary pull me out of my meeting. The kids were great.

Dad was admitted into Beth Israel and in a few days went into their hospice. My brother came over and we sang a few hymns to see if he would rouse. He didn't and died in the night. He was with us from October until March. One of the last things he said before he lapsed into a coma was, "I'm ready to go." Then he added, "It went fast."

What went fast was virtually the whole Twentieth Century, from 1905 to 1996. With him went the memory of the old gas lighters, penny loaves of bread, crystal sets, and horseless carriages. Most especially he carried away the detailed memories of my brother's and my early days. Our babyhood was his prime. "Oh, Daddy," we would say dismissively when he tried to tell us what precocious and funny tots we had been. I am grateful that he was undaunted.

15

DEPRESSION

By now I was worn down by the struggle. For thirteen years I had to deal with the tribulations that come with a special needs child: where she should go to school, where she should get treatment, how to explain her oddness to strangers, how to shore up her skills so that she could fledge.

Could she fledge? That was the question that plagued me. High school was nearly over. Was there a place for her in the adult world and if there was, did I have what it took to find it?

And then I had to support us. Sometimes I would think, *I can't do my job any more.* Patience at work and patience at home. As I fell asleep at night, I imagined losing my job, and then losing the apartment, and then wrapping Tammy and me in blankets and lying against the buildings on Fourteenth Street with all the others who had lost everything.

And yet, I wouldn't have lost everything. I would have Tammy with me. And if we were warm, wrapped in our blankets, then okay. We were okay. I could sleep.

How the great have fallen. What happened to my flowery bower and the lily pond?

Throughout her life, all the boys and friendships and relationships, Tammy suffered deep depressions. She spent her money on coffee and cigarettes. She told her therapist that she wanted to melt into her coffee. The pattern we had earlier, where she went to bed and then I at last had some time to get something done, was over. She stayed up later than I did, and I didn't know what she was doing. Tammy missed her brothers after Shaunie sent first Matt and then Martin to Florida to live with the man in Jacksonville who had adopted the oldest brother, Chris. In the morning, Tammy would often leave me a letter with suicidal overtones and plans to drop out of school.

One letter read:

> There has been a lot of problems in my life. I know you don't think so but it's true. My life is really messed up right now and I think it would be best if I just leave for a while, so that is what I am doing. I just think that I am doing the right thing. I am not trying to hurt you so please don't think I am. I love you very much and I always will. You are very special to me. I just think I need some time alone. I don't know how long but I do know that I have to leave. I am very sorry but this is something that I have to do and I have to do this alone. I promise that I will come back someday I just don't know when. Please don't call the police.
>
> I will come back, I love you with all my heart.

She signed this letter Tammy Gonzalez, which was a good sign. She signed other letters Tammy Shaughnessy. In those letters, she expressed more anger and alienation from me. Often the theme was her imminent departure. But she had no place to go and always ended up coming home.

She was right to suspect me of not believing how miserable she felt. I was busy teaching a full load while chairing the department. I also wanted to be a useful contributor to language education. I devised a project for eight curriculum units – for every level from fifth grade to AP on *la francophonie*, the French speaking world outside of France. My own stress was getting out of hand. I was exhausted from managing Tammy and from the months of caring for my father. Her growing up years were coming to a close and together we could not come up with a plan for her future. I pushed her to take more Sign Language courses with me, to take a course in hip-hop dance, and to keep up with her skating. The psychologist Bob Newhart used to play would tell his patients, "Just snap out of it." That's what I wanted. I wanted her to "Just snap out of it."

The summer before, to relieve the pressure, I sent her to a Special Needs Camp in North Carolina. They piled the kids into a van for an exciting trip to the Florida Keys and Dry Tortugas where she scuba-dived and snorkeled. I pampered myself with a week at a spa. This summer, I sent her to that camp for a trip to Belize and Guatemala. I went to Martinique and Guadeloupe. I came back with material and ideas for my curriculum. She came back revved up and full of stories, but the elation didn't last.

I passed the missives along to the therapist. Tammy wrote:

> I am thinking of being a drop-out. What I am trying to say is I am thinking of dropping out of school. Look I know you want me to get an education in High School but the truth and the fact is I can't handle my own life. So just how am I supposed to handle school. I don't want to get you mad or worry at what I'm doing. I like school a lot but I can't handle it and until I can handle my own life I can't school. Everything in my life is going so fast and I just can't handle it. That's why I would like to kill myself. More and more each day I feel more and more depressed about school and my life and when I look back at things I would just like to die. Please understand. Right now I don't like my life very much.
>
> Love,
>
> Tammy

This note caused genuine alarm at St. Vincent's. I, however, was not alarmed; I didn't believe this note was about suicide. My view was that she wanted something that cost money. I was waiting to find out what it was. The psychiatrist met with her and prescribed an anti-depressant. I wish I could say that the pill did the trick. It turned out that a pricy class ring was on her mind. I bought the ring, and her mood lifted. Sometimes—often—money worked.

So I knew her and knew that her depressions did not come explained in a note. They came in sullen silences, in forgetting to bathe, in long feral faces, in dangerous fasts. They were not about school or people she knew. They were dank pits of hopelessness and angst. She was lost in the slough of despond. Therapy followed by sushi therapy kept her from losing her way entirely. I saw what misery looks like, and I saw that I couldn't fix it. This was my sorrow: all the good will in the world couldn't fix it.

At last a break. I was blessed. Water from the font of mercy touched my fevered brow. Friends initiated a sabbatical program, and I won the award with my curriculum project. It provided a semester off with full pay and benefits. For the fall of Tammy's senior year, I would stay at home and devise lessons that would crack open the world for my students, revealing to them the expanse of the francophone world, showing them that French was a worldwide language with a thriving African, North American and Caribbean literature and music. For twenty-eight years, I had been teaching at Friends. My textbook, *Louis Souris et ses amis*, was cobbled together from lessons I was making up every day for my fifth and sixth graders. The leisure to focus entirely on a project was a gift from the gods. Lift up your heart! Lift up your voice! Rejoice! (You can take the girl out of the church, but you can't take the hymnal out of the girl).

Despite the vicissitudes of her emotions, Tammy managed to pass all the Regents Competency Tests and would get a regular diploma.

I spent my days discovering African and Caribbean music. I found a Louisiana song that had made its way to Africa to be converted from Zydeco to reggae. I put Aristide's inaugural address, the first ever delivered in Haitian Creole, side by side with its French version so students could see linguistic parallels. I found African proverbs expressed in French, which held ancient wisdom. Tammy came home every night to a happy and rested mother. We both perked up.

At the last minute before graduation the Lowell School informed me that Tammy had been absent so often she would not graduate. Now you tell me! I said, please, there must be a way. What did she owe? What work did she have to do? For her years there it had never seemed to me that there was any academic expectation. When she first began, I asked why there was no home-work. The principal told me that if they assigned it, the kids wouldn't do it. There was no math for her to take so they gave her an intellectually disabled child to tutor. The kids went out to smoke every hour or so. I wondered how many days she had not made it to school or had just bugged out during the smoking break.

The art class seemed to be the main obstacle. They informed me that had rarely attended, if at all. If she wrote a report on an artist, she could get credit and graduate. I did an over-the-phone kowtow.

As soon as Tammy got home I asked her who her favorite artist was. She said, "Monet."

I handed her a notebook, got in a cab with her, and went to the Museum of Modern Art. I plunked her in front of the huge water lily canvases and said, "Write. Describe what you see."

She wrote and observed and looked at books. Her report was the only academic achievement of note in her high school years. At the graduation, the art teacher commented favorably. I said that I wished she had had more opportunities to get involved with a project. But too late for that.

Her brothers Matt and Chris were visiting Shaunie the weekend of Tammy's graduation. We piled into the Toyota and took the ride up the BQE to the Grand Central. By now I could write a book with instructions on how to prepare for every single exit-only on the trek. Tammy and Auric were among the six students to receive a regular (not IEP) diploma. We sat through the speeches and now a teacher was talking about an exemplary student. This student would receive the award for community service for her faithful and professional tutoring of a student in math. The recipient was none other than Tammy Gonzalez.

Matt and I jumped up and hugged each other, drowning out the applause with our whuh-hoos.

PART IV
1998-2007

16

LAUNCHING TAMMY

Launching Tammy into the adult world became my obsession. She wasn't working and she wasn't going to school. Therapy, classes in American Sign Language, and a tiny job as assistant in the nursery at church on Sunday mornings were the only sources of structure in her life.

My idea, of course, was that she would go to college. Everybody I knew had gone to college. I made her sit for the SAT's. I guess I knew they were too hard for her, but I felt I needed a baseline so I would know where to start. Also, denial is a chronic condition. She took them at Friends Seminary. A colleague was proctoring.

"I don't know, Sue," I said. "She might not have the patience to sit through the whole thing."

"Don't worry. She'll be fine."

She did stay through the whole thing and even boasted to me that she finished before some of the Friends kids she had been a classmate with when they were little. I knew she must have raced through not really focusing on the questions. Years before, when she went to Friends, the lower school had an afternoon off, but the rest of the school still had classes. I asked her to sit quietly at the back of my classroom. My most advanced students were doing a multiple-choice exercise on some tough rules about the sequence of tenses.

I gave a copy to Tammy and told her to pick A. B, C, or D on each question. She pondered the letters while the students pondered the verbs. Was the conditional perfect required in this clause? Tammy didn't know a word of French, but she did know the alphabet. She thought long and hard about whether to mark B or C. I lost all faith in multiple choice when she scored as well as the kids who had been studying French for the past seven years.

This time, however, she scored at a percentile so low that undoubtedly college would be too much of a challenge.

However, there are colleges and colleges, and the Lowell School guided their students toward a place where they could succeed. Tammy got into two colleges, but she put her foot down. She would not go.

"Tammy, you'll learn things. You'll make friends. "

"No. What part of 'no' do you not understand?"

I didn't know where to turn. I remembered that Donna had worked in a sheltered workshop years before, and I thought that this might work for Tammy. I couldn't find any for people like her who were not intellectually disabled. We looked at a residential facility uptown for people with mental health problems. So far as we could tell, the inhabitants either abused drugs or had serious illnesses like schizophrenia. It was a depressing place even for people who didn't have problems with depression. I was depressed.

Someone in the church needed office help. She went for an interview and told them that her greatest strength was her knowledge of the alphabet. (She did not get the job.)

We went to see a campus on the border of New York and Vermont for young adults with conditions like Tammy's. We liked the bucolic setting and the independence offered the residents. It was a cool summer day and we both felt that winter there might be brutal. The site included a restaurant across the street where the residents worked as waitresses or bussing tables. We ate lunch there and both noticed that most of the work was done by staff. Room and board was very pricy and neither of us fell in love with the place.

The problem for Tammy was that she was so nearly normal. I was dismayed that there were places for the delusional, the addicted and the intellectually disabled but no place for my Tammy.

As soon as they stopped seeing each other every day at school, Tammy and Auric drifted apart. Though it was none of my business, I missed Auric. It was like having a nephew pulled out of your family. Floyd was waiting in the wings. Tammy said, "I'm VERY attracted to Floyd." I could see why. When I first met him at the Halloween party I thought he was beautiful. He probably wouldn't have liked that word. He was a testosterone driven macho male. But his skin was milky white, and at the party his hair tumbled about his head in dark, unruly waves and curls. I guess he was short, but you would never think of him as short because his shoulders were massive and his bearing, larger-than-life. His wide, wide smile made you want to love him.

Now, though, the curls were gone. Floyd had aged out of his group home. Within a month of living on the street he did a stint at Riker's Island. His crime was holding a bag with drugs so that the true seller could keep his own hands clean. Literally, left holding the bag. They shaved his head at Riker's.

Floyd was in the same boat as Tammy. He would have been normal had it not been for the life imposed on him by abandonment and the system. Another "nearly normal." Where were people like them to turn—people not really qualified for college and not able to present themselves for a job without support?

The place in upstate New York sparked a new fantasy. I would acquire a brownstone in Alphabet City. Downstairs in the storefront, there would be a coffee shop. Upstairs the marginally disabled young adults would have rooms with kitchenettes. A wonderful graduate of Dunkin Donuts University, who would also possess social work skills, would manage this center of all that is cool. He/she would teach Tammy and Mercedes and Ivette how to make scrumptious brownies and macadamia nut chocolate chip cookies that would become the rage of the Lower East Side. Floyd would learn how to brew up dynamite lattes and cappuccinos. They would become experts in keeping accurate books and publicizing their wares. One young nearly normal guitar player would take charge of Friday night musical events. The Coffee Shop would be a hub.

Alas, I'm a dreamer.

When they released him from Riker's, Floyd, along with a few other down-and-out young men, found shelter in the apartment of the very dealer, referred to only as "the Punisher," responsible for his incarceration. More than once the luckless boy came over with black eyes and swollen lips. My friend on the Eleventh floor said, "Oh, poor Floyd. I saw him in the elevator. What happened?"

He would never tell. He just adopted the stock line, "You should see the other guy." He couldn't toss the line off lightly, though; he was seething with anger. I said, "Floyd, you can't stay there. You'd be better off in a homeless shelter."

"The Punisher would never let me leave."

"Floyd, you can leave."

"The last person who tried to leave ended up dead."

"Mom, you heard about that kid who was killed."

I'd heard about a recent murder of a young man in Alphabet City. Floyd and Tammy both assured me that this death was the Punisher's work.

"Oh no." I said. "We've got to get you out of there. Maybe we should call the police."

"Marge, no!" Floyd was emphatic. "He didn't do it himself. He got someone else to do it. "

"Mom, everybody knows that. Don't get Floyd killed!"

I was alarmed, not so much because I thought Floyd was in imminent danger, but because his life was so precarious. How was it that Floyd was released from his group home with no lodging waiting? I called Jewish

Children's Charities, the same agency that had been so astonished that Tammy didn't have a child. The social worker assigned to Scott was also in charge of Floyd's case. He told me that they had no further responsibility for Floyd. I said, "What about a moral responsibility? He's in danger. He has no place to live." He described Floyd as "grandiose," and said, "Floyd did not cooperate with his exit plan."

I bet he didn't. Floyd had dreams of acquiring wealth in the computer world. He certainly would have resisted paths that seemed beneath his dreams. Tammy seemed odd to people, but not Floyd. He had charm. I felt sure that with guidance he could get a good job and work his way up. But no one had taken the trouble to guide him, at least not the way family would, not the way I would for Tammy. She wasn't cooperating with her "exit plan" either but I wasn't throwing her out on the mean streets.

But his social skills were a thin veneer that hid a boy who had suffered abominable parenting. When I tried to draw him out about his life, I discovered he had a shaky sense of the chronology. He knew that at one point he had spent months, maybe a year, in a mental facility. He came away with a monumental distrust of psychologists and psychiatrists. "They mess with your mind." I wondered if for all that time he was sent repeatedly to a padded room for the most innocuous infraction. A few days in the locked ward at St. Vincent's had been enough for Tammy.

He had three brothers. "My brothers and I, we raised ourselves. My dad was in jail and my mom was almost never home. We cooked, we did everything." Nervous laughs punctuated his narration. So that he wouldn't cry. So that I wouldn't know how awful it was.

Once he was in the system, he suffered the crushing disappointment of waiting and waiting to be adopted and loved and cared for and never getting what he longed for.

So now he was thrust out into the streets where a criminal predator was waiting.

I inherited a little money from my father and took it into my head that I needed a country place. Then I realized I wouldn't know what to do in the country. I wanted to be on the water. That was it—I wanted a water view. Now that I knew my way around Queens a little, I settled on a condo in College Point, near LaGuardia Airport. It looked right out on the East River, where it widens before the Whitestone Bridge. The occasional swan strayed into my little inlet. The complex was next to the lovely MacNeil Park, with huge shade trees and an esplanade right along the water. I saw myself spending summers there, in air-conditioned comfort, and eventually making it my retirement home. There was even a pool. The normal flight path meant that planes noiselessly flew by my balcony in route to land. I imagined myself getting familiar with the daily flights. I saw myself saying, "Ah, there's the 2:30 from Rochester."

Floyd was at our place in Stuyvesant Town every day. Then one day he didn't come over. Then the next and the next. I was worried. Tammy seemed strangely unconcerned. After about a week he called. He said he was back at Riker's. He explained to Tammy what had happened. He had gone to the police to report the theft of his cell phone, and his own name popped up on the computer. It appeared he had neglected to visit his probation officer from his first trip to jail. We spent our weekends in Queens. From the condo balcony we could see the George Washington Bridge in the distance. In the foreground, we saw Riker's. We knew he was in there.

For a month or two we heard nothing from Floyd. Then one morning before church, Tammy and I were sitting in the Croissanterie on 34th St. A very familiar face, now with a stubble of beard, passed by. "Oh my God! Floyd!"

Tammy ran out to pull him in to join us. He had been released, placed in a shelter near the Tri-Borough Bridge and given a job. He had come to this area looking for Tammy – he figured he'd find her at the church.

"Floyd, this is fantastic; you can make a fresh start. At last the powers that be are helping you. The Punisher doesn't know anything about where you are now," I said.

To my relief, he agreed.

So now he was back and hanging out with Tammy day and night. He came over one more time with a split lip and black eye. This time he had gotten in a scuffle when someone tried to steal his shoes as he slept in the shelter. Fighting over shoes. A Beckett parable had pushed its way into this poor boy's real life. He was forced to sleep with his shoes on.

One Friday shortly after his release from Riker's, Floyd came with us to Queens in the old Toyota heading for a sushi place we had found in College Point. In the course of the conversation he said he had quit the job. I couldn't believe my ears.

"What do you mean?"

"It wasn't very good and . . .."

"Are you saying that you were handed a job on a silver platter but you were just too good for it?"

I was overtaken with fury, a sudden and virulent burst of temper which my husband (what husband, you ask. Yes, there will be a husband) refers to as The Wrath of Marge. "Are you kidding? A job is just handed you and you think it's OK to walk away?" I pulled over. "Get out of the car."

"But."

"Get out. Now."

He got out. We were somewhere in one of Queens ethnic pockets. It could have been a Bangladeshi neighborhood or a Guyanese one. Or Indian or Pakistani. I didn't care. I agreed with the social worker. Grandiose.

Tammy was too shocked to say a word. Through force of habit I went straight to the condo instead of the restaurant. Anyway, neither of us was hungry. I puttered away working off my anger. Tammy kept a low profile.

I went out on the balcony and noticed it was raining lightly. I looked out toward the George Washington Bridge, but it was engulfed in mist. When I looked over to the east, I was startled. On the other side of the inlet between our complex and the park, I saw a white mournful face, framed in a hoodie, staring at me. Oh lord, he walked here through the drizzle. I thought of my mother's words, "You know what I told you about putting yourself in the other person's place? Well forget it. You do it too much." But he looked so forlorn. Where do you go to learn to be a hard ass? I crumbled.

"Tammy, go over there and get that jerk and tell him he needs to come up with an employment plan."

My one last hope for Tammy was VESID– Vocational Educational Services for Individuals with Disabilities. VESID was the sprawling state agency for rehabilitative services for the disabled. There was a branch in the very building where years before she had met with Julie for speech therapy. Tammy was placed in a typing class although she already knew how to type. I figured they would assess her skills and place her in a class that fit, but after two weeks, Tammy began to complain. "They won't let me off the home keys."

"What are you saying?"

"I'm bored. Ever since I got there I've been on the home keys."

"Tammy, wait a minute. Are you saying you're typing the same eight letters over and over?"

"Yup."

"Well, Tammy, the teacher must not realize that you can type."

"I keep telling her I can type, but she says, 'This is what you're assigned. This is what you have to do.'"

She was twenty. I was going to let her handle this. But no, I got called in. "We have other students who would work in our program, others who would really appreciate the opportunity to be here." 'This doesn't meet my daughter's needs' wouldn't work here. I felt as though I were in the little chairs of the Friends Seminary classroom when she was counseled out. This time Tammy was kicked out of a program for the disabled.

I racked my brain. What new prospect could I uncover? I thought of her tiny job at the church in the nursery. Maybe she could – but I was stumped. I was a taut spring; I felt the urgency of the situation in my neck and in my muscles. She was a young adult but until she found something to do, she was my child.

While I was desperately trying to regroup, she disappeared. One night she didn't come home all night. Where could she be? Floyd couldn't take her to his homeless shelter. Could the Punisher have resurfaced? I was so frantic I went over to the police precinct. I said that she had autism. That was sort of a lie I guess, but if I'd said PDD-NOS, they wouldn't have known what I was talking about. And it was on the spectrum. They thought it sounded serious for a person with autism to be missing. A male and female officer took me in their squad car, and we went roaming the streets of Alphabet City. I told them that she and her homeless boyfriend often spent time in a place called "Alt Coffee" on Avenue B. The female officer went in and came out saying that they had been in and out of there numerous times all night.

The police promised to keep an eye out for her and gave me the option of an arbitration meeting to discuss things with both Tammy and Floyd once they turned up. I figured I could always cancel it later so I took them up on the offer. This was a way to compel them to talk things over with me. The police said that Alt Coffee would call the precinct as soon as Tammy and Floyd appeared, and they would serve Tammy and Floyd with a summons or invitation or whatever it was to meet for this chat or arbitration or whatever it was.

When she got the summons, she came home to confront me with a fair degree of heat. "What's this? What the heck is this?'

"I didn't know where you were. I was worried. I wanted to make sure I would see you. Don't do anything crazy, Tammy."

Then a week later, before the date of the chat/arbitration, she left again. She didn't come home all night. I didn't realize she was gone until the morning when I was getting ready to go to work. I thought the police would say I was a nuisance if I went to them again. She did come home the other time. She would come back again. I went to school. After my last class, I rushed home to find no trace of her. The thought of her traipsing through deserted parks and sordid neighborhoods with homeless Floyd made me fly out on my own search. I forgot she was a needle in a haystack. I wanted her back. All of my being distilled into this one urgent need. Find Tammy.

One day I had a child. The next, I found myself driving north on Manhattan's Second Avenue, against the traffic, the wrong way on a busy one-way road, blinded by tears, searching for her, brakes screeching, horns sounding all around me, and finally a siren and a kind policeman listening to me moan that my daughter was missing. The officer tried to help, but finally he let me know, disabled or not, she was an adult.

17
YOU DON'T GET IT, MOM?

She didn't come home. She didn't call. I tried to go on with life. I went to work every day. I don't know how I did it. I cried on the shoulder of Anne and Annette, my two closest colleagues. Anne remembered how it was. "Dearest Marge, You were terribly terribly distraught. I often wondered how you could continue with all the emotional upset."

Maybe you could say I should be happy. My little bird had flown. This was what I wanted. Turns out it wasn't exactly what I wanted. Homelessness was like royalty – you could marry into it. I wanted her to have a place in the world. Joining the homeless seemed to me the very opposite of what I wanted. It was having no place at all.

I was a robot teaching French. My worry went into my body. I felt as though the back of my head was in a vice. I thought I was having a breakdown and then I thought of how inconvenient it would be to have a breakdown. Annette looked at me and said, "Marge, you're not doing well. You really should get some help," and then she told me about another friend with an addiction-prone daughter who had gone to Families Anonymous. "Keep it in mind. It really helped her."

I hoped Tammy and Floyd would feel they had to show up for the meeting. Could she just leave and I would never see her again?

I went to church and, in the middle of a hymn, burst into tears. Another member, Jennifer, was sitting beside me. She took my hand and led me out to a bench in front of the church. "Tammy's left," I blubbered. "I don't know where she is." Though a reserved Brit who didn't really know me very well,

Jennifer put her arms around me. I was too miserable to be mortified, which heaven knows, I am in retrospect.

I got hold of myself enough to thank Jennifer and went to splash water on my face. It suddenly occurred to me that maybe Tammy had come to her job in the nursery. I went over to the brownstone that served as the Sunday School building. There she was. She looked beautiful. Her hair was clean and tended, still wavy from a perm. I felt the way I always felt when she came home late – so relieved that she was alive and well and so furious that she had let me worry so.

"Hi, Mom."

"Tammy, please tell me you haven't done anything stupid like getting married."

She looked at me blankly. I feared that was just what she had done. When she said, "No," I felt a burst of irrational hope that things would go back where they were.

The arbitration was in a dark windowless basement in lower Manhattan. I got there first. The setting was as bleak as my mood. I was alone in the cramped corridor, furnished with a few folding, metallic chairs, that served as a waiting room. There was nothing to read, not even a flyer.

The facilitator emerged from a little conference room. An older woman, she let me know that she had no power. She was just there to help keep the conversation going. Tammy and Floyd arrived, Floyd acting more full of himself than usual. He greeted the lady and me, smiling with overbearing pleasantness. Oh yeah, he was the man. Tammy was hiding under her hair. She left all the talking to Floyd. What had he done with my sassy girl? She acted like a classic submissive female, wholly subsumed in her man's identity. He was the prince and I was Rapunzel's witch. I didn't have a prayer.

We settled around a grey table in a grey room, barely large enough to contain the sterile furniture. The first thing Floyd said was "Now that we're married. . ."

I didn't hear the rest of the sentence. My heartbeat was thundering in my ears.

So this was how I found out. In a casual dependent clause. My usual instinct to maintain my composure at all cost failed to kick in. Only I didn't feel as though I would cry. I felt as though I would lose consciousness and need to be resuscitated. I guess no one was looking at me or they would have called the paramedics. The life I wanted for Tammy, the life I had worked and longed for exploded into smoke. She had thrown away her life. Leonardo da Vinci couldn't have felt more devastated if he saw the Mona Lisa burst into flame. Or rather he couldn't have felt more devastated if he saw the model for the Mona Lisa blow up before he had a chance to paint her. Why did they do it this way? Why didn't they wait and have a wedding after they had made a start in the adult world? My daughter got married and I wasn't even there. No veil, no pretty dress. She probably wore torn jeans with a denim work shirt.

Floyd chirped on with his characteristic laugh about how he would go into computer repair and Tammy would become a manicurist. Oh and they had gone to a photographer to get 8 by 10 glossies so that in the meantime they could do some modeling. Ah yes, he was in charge; he would take care of everything. Old guard, step aside. I sat struggling to concoct a way to turn back the hands of time.

The moderator asked if she could talk with the couple alone. I cooled my heels in the claustrophobic corridor. I hated them, most particularly I hated Floyd. They came out and then left. No "Congratulations" from me. No "see you later, Mom" from her. The woman told me that the kids needed and wanted my support. Really? I had gotten the impression that I was the enemy. I said that I wanted the marriage annulled.

Tammy came to church the next week. I drove her back to their shelter in Bedford-Stuyvesant. Then week after week I took her to lunch on Sundays, to Mindy's Kosher Deli or the café in the courtyard of the Morgan Library or Au Bon Pain. Then I drove her back ranting, through the Queens Midtown Tunnel and down the BQE, about how wrong this all was, that she wasn't homeless, that she had a bedroom in Stuyvesant Town and another one in our condo in Queens to boot. I screamed, negotiating the endless double-parked vans of Flatbush Avenue, about jobs, training, income, and responsibility. She watched the traffic. I yelled, threading my way through the narrow, littered streets of Bed-Sty, that I hoped he was giving her good orgasms for all the aggravation. She was mum.

I was the trustee of her disability money. Every week I transferred a fourth of it into her account so that it would last the month. Floyd and Tammy went to the Social Security office and changed things so that Floyd became the trustee. Years later when she needed a trustee again, I discovered it would never be me. On the record they had both said I was stealing her money.

I refused to speak to Floyd. Someone suggested that they were probably in love. I scoffed at the thought. My view was that he had manipulated her because married people got better shelters. Single men were put out of their cots onto the street at the crack of dawn, while couples got rooms with locks. Many times, Tammy and I had volunteered at the shelter for men at our church. The men would file in at about 8 PM, then gather at a table, and help themselves to white bread and American cheese. Conversations with us put dim lights into their weary faces. In the morning, after they left, we put the cots away so the rooms could once again be used for committee meetings and Sunday School.

When I learned what an upgrade marriage provided, I protested to the authorities. "I'm angry at the Coalition for the Homeless," I wrote. "I'm angry at the shelter system. Why didn't you call the mother of this clearly emotionally disabled girl? Didn't it matter that she had a loving home with a room still full of stuffed animals and hundreds of Barbies? Isn't one supposed to be *homeless* to get these services? Or are you there to help kids when their mothers get in the way of their sex lives because they believe people should get jobs and earn some money in advance of holy wedlock?" I called hotlines to tell them I wanted to kidnap her back and annul the marriage. One hot line person said, "You're broken hearted."

"Never mind my heart," I snapped. "Let me finish raising my daughter.'"

But the suggestion of love kept seeping into my consciousness. I began to wonder if he did love her. Life flowed on; their marriage endured. Intermittently I saw myself as one of Moliere's ludicrous blocking parents, she whose rigid stand produces all the comedy. Someone else told me that when your child marries, you have to suck it up.

So I invited them to a potluck and sing-along at the church that spring. Jennifer was across the groaning board from us as we loaded our plates. "This is Floyd, my son-in-law," I said. "So nice to meet you, Floyd." He flushed from happiness. Then I remembered how much I had liked him when I first met him and what a beautiful boy I thought he was when he came to our Halloween Party. The invitation had read "For Teens and Their Parents," but of course he had no parent to bring. How had I missed how much this boy craved a family? Well, now he had a wife. I guess he also had a mother-in-law.

I loved teaching French and could scarcely imagine life without a regular paycheck. I was the chair of a well-regarded foreign language department. Yet I had failed to convey to my only child, the major focus of my life for the previous fifteen years, that gainful employment was the ticket to freedom and dignity. After all those years of shepherding her to therapists of various stripes, myriad attempts to remediate her issues with activities and pills, new efforts to forget remediation and play to her strengths, and countless struggles with the Board of Education, I had a daughter who did not see a path forward that included work. That's when she told me impatiently, "You don't get it. You get married and you have a baby."

I never, never saw this coming. I saw her body in space intelligence, her dance, her skating, her brilliance at sign language, even her skill as a manicurist. I couldn't fathom that she didn't want to use her talents to make a mark on the world and provide herself an income that would pull her above the poverty line. But as usual, it came down to a question of who needed to be fixed. I got so upset – I still get upset – when I see a kid with Down syndrome working at Lowe's or the autistic kid delivering the mail in my husband's old job. I take it personally. Those parents were better advocates for their children than I was for Tammy. She would be good at bagging groceries at Publix, but I couldn't make it happen. Not even that. I put it on me that someday she would be a crotchety old lady who couldn't pay her electric bill. My optimistic buoyancy took a pounding. I imagined her diving into new lows of misery without her creature comforts like AC and TV and Wi-Fi because I couldn't figure out how to make opportunity come knocking.

18

PAUL

That summer, with a lump sum from SSI, they rented their own place on Flatbush Avenue in Brooklyn, a second-floor walk-up over a tombstone shop ("our gravestones – to die for"), and Tammy got pregnant. My sister-in–law said, "Congratulations, Marge, you're sixty years old and you're having a baby."

I was going to France for a few weeks, and Tammy and Floyd agreed to take care of the cat. I took Tinacat over and discovered that they were about to be evicted for not paying rent. I paid it "just this one time," mainly for the cat.

After I returned, Floyd called me late one night. Tammy was moaning in pain, and he didn't know what to do. I told him to go to an emergency room and to keep me posted. She ended up admitted to Beth Israel with a serious urinary tract infection. Floyd demanded a cot for himself in her room. I saw his anxiety, his will to protect her, and his inability to leave her side to go to the job he'd had for two days, mopping up at a McDonald's. He grew up in group homes and special needs boarding schools. No one loved him except Tammy. I paid their rent again and offered him the place in Queens.

Tammy and Floyd left the roach-infested, noise-polluted apartment in Brooklyn to await the baby in the condo. I wrote up elaborate documents, which I made Tammy and Floyd sign. I agreed to provide a home for one year and to pay tuition for courses, and they agreed to take care of the place, pay the electric and cable bills, and work on their educations. We signed the contract with formality. Every provision was initialed and witnessed. And then we renewed it because, as my friends noticed before I did, a year was not enough.

Then they did their best. The second Tammy knew she was pregnant she stopped smoking. She abstained from all alcohol to the point of inquiring if the dish in a restaurant was made with wine. She was taking no chances.

I couldn't give up. I found a certificate program in ASL at Hunter College. Since it was part of Continuing Education, there were no admission requirements. Tammy and I took it together, and she didn't miss a class until she was nine months pregnant. Then she came back when Paul was just a month old. She was excellent at signing; once again, there was Tammy, and then there was the rest of the class. Literally. I'm a language teacher, but I really struggled with comprehension; Tammy caught on in a heartbeat. Her talent filled me with hope. I imagined her working as a paraprofessional, sitting with a mainstreamed deaf child. Floyd found a course that would lead to A+ certification in computer repair. He kept up with it while working full time at BJ's.

My new mission in life became to push Floyd into the work force. A week before baby Paul was born, Floyd lost his job at BJ's. ("That's okay, Floyd, you just have to get back out there and get another job.")

The baby was late. They finally decided to induce labor, again at Beth Israel. As I walked the two blocks from Friends Seminary, I spotted a serenely happy Tammy crossing First Avenue, coming from Stuyvesant Town. Floyd showed up, and I went home figuring that this would take a while. I knew less than Butterfly McQueen about birthin' babies, but I 'd seen how long it takes on TV – hours, days (unless of course you are stuck in an elevator in which cases delivery is remarkably fast and requires the aid of the only other passenger, usually a neurotic adolescent.) Luckily she was not in an elevator; this would take a while.

The phone woke me. Floyd said I had better get over there fast. I ran to the hospital through a light February snow. When I walked into the room, the doctor said, "Are you her mother?"

"Yes."

"Thank goodness. Now push."

"I wouldn't push until you got here, Mom."

So fast! A few good pushes with the doctor's urgent voice saying "Don't stop! No, no, don't stop. Push!" and then the baby's cry. I couldn't see the mightily pissed off infant through the back of the doctor. "Okay, Dad," he said to Floyd, "Here's your job." I heard Floyd chuckling along with the shrieks of the baby and the ohs and ahs of the nurse. "Cut the umbilical cord."

Then the little bundle with the angry red face and the adorable cap was in the Plexiglas bassinet in front of me. Tammy was getting some stitches and crying, "I want to see him."

But I was the one who saw him. "Shush baby, it's okay. Welcome to the world." I said.

"Don't comfort him," said the nurse. "He needs to exercise his lungs."

Would he have a clue about what comforting was? I just looked at him and hoped he would revise his opinion of life on planet earth.

Everyone talks about the finger and the toes, but what about those perfect minuscule fingernails? Floyd was with me looking and beaming. We both felt the miracle. Truly, I do not understand why people turn to the otherworldly for the holy. This world is enough.

I could feel Tammy's urgent longing to see him. She was still crying for him, and he and I were already old friends.

I love how the characters in fairy tales transform. The humble become princesses. Perhaps the wicked witch would now become the fairy god-mother. Paul would grow up enveloped in my good wishes. This time, I would be those three good fairies, all wrapped up into one. I would bestow health, long life, and happiness. As much as I could, I would.

Many years before, as I walked up Park Avenue, a cab hit a lady right in front of me. I looked around. There was no one on the sidewalk but me. I would have to step off the curb and be the Samaritan. I would be late for my therapy session and the encouragement to finish my dissertation and find a man. Against all odds, the lady was French, the cabbie was a French-speaking Algerian, and the third person on the scene was *moi*. A doctor came running out of one of the offices and asked, "What hurts?"

"Qu'est-ce qui vous fait mal, Madame?" I said.

"C'est le poignet droit."

So I could tell the doctor it was her right wrist, and he could put a splint on it and run back before the ambulance got there. I would tell this story year in and year out to my French classes (minus my own destination, of course) to illustrate the utility of language study.

Now when it came to mind, it showed something else. I looked around and there was only me. Who else would buoy this young couple? The dread empty nest syndrome was a transition I was unlikely to ever have to cope with. I wanted my daughter back? Well it looked as though I was going to get her along with two more hungry mouths. While my peers were cruising up the Danube or visiting the Taj Mahal, I would be reading *In the Night Kitchen* and singing nightly lullabies. I would be insuring that Floyd got up in time for work and that Tammy took her meds. I was stuck. So why was I smiling?

More importantly, I was a fool. As Annette suggested, I went to Families Anonymous. I listened to the horrific tragedies of good people whose children were lost to drugs, children who (if they were alive or talked at all with their parents) came around only to beg for money or to steal. The full weight of my nonsensical position hit me. My twenty-year-old daughter got married. Boohoo.

Very slowly, my anger with the Coalition for the Homeless abated. To me, there is still no question that they were terribly wrong in aiding and abetting this irresponsible marriage. What if I hadn't been there? What if little Paulie had landed in the system. Another generation would have been lost. I am be-side myself when I think of the harm he would have suffered. From October until May of 2000, the young couple had a room of their own. Mom's litany of education and work was clearly false. Food and lodging came free. Every month my daughter got her SSI payment, and it seemed pretty good with the necessities out of the way. One month the money could get them some Kmart wedding rings. The next they could buy a TV, and the next, a VCR. Since real-ity proved me wrong on the work ethic, why should they pay the slightest mind to my appeals to wait to have a baby until they could afford one?

"Just because my grandson is the rising sun in the east," I wrote the Coalition in an unmailed letter (my mind was in perpetual conversation with them) "and just because he jumps up and down in his little play seat with its stimulating activity tray, squealing with glee and flailing his arms like an ecstatic twittering machine when grandma comes into view, don't think I forgive you."

But for my own sake, I did forgive them. Baby Paul was perfect. His ador-ableness, his sturdy finger hold, his baby boy stubbornness, his sheer delight in life, eloquently, and definitively refuted any argument for waiting.

Tammy and I had finished three levels of ASL when Hunter informed us that there would be no class in Deaf Culture, the last requirement for the certificate, because we were the only two who signed up. I wrote a letter to the president of the college ("Go to the top") protesting that I had sunk a wad of cash into this program for two students. By gum—Shaunie was right! We were given a course by a brilliant deaf professor, just the two of us, and since we were not at a high enough level to understand a lecture course conducted entirely in Sign, we also had our own interpreter. This class required us to go to Deaf events around the city. We were usually the only hearing people at plays and parties except for some of the deaf people's children, who pumped up the volume to the music with nary a raised eyebrow from their parents.

I began to lobby for ASL as a way to meet the language requirement at Friends. Tammy had been waived out of every Spanish class she began; yet here she shone. I began to amass evidence that some learning disabled kids, because of their confusion when presented with letters, are astute at reading visual, bodily clues. We waived the language requirement for a boy of surpassing sweetness, who was null in Spanish, when he was in the seventh grade. Later, in the tenth grade he begged me let him take French. He said he wouldn't mind being with kids who were four years younger. He struggled until the pain was too great, and he dropped out. This same boy came back from college and couldn't wait to seek me out to let me know that he had taken ASL and excelled. It met his needs; it met Tammy's needs. I also liked the idea that we would be reaching out to people within our own borders who could not learn to speak and process oral English. Despite the passion of my proposal, the Curriculum committee nixed it. Dang it, I forgot to go to the top.

Floyd picked himself up from the loss of the job at BJ's and almost immediately went to work at the local supermarket. When he got the certificate, we celebrated by dining at the Life Café, a funky spot in Alphabet City, which was replicated as part of the set of Rent. Paul slept contentedly in his carrier on the floor. For a shining moment we were a proud and happy family. We laughed and toasted each other, savoring the success. Life was sweet.

Floyd began a course for N+ certification in network repair. But things started to fall apart at the supermarket. He fought with his boss. Through all the years of childhood when he was not parented adequately, he somehow managed to get the message that he was worth something, that he could not be bullied, that he deserved respect. I tried to tell him that you have to make an exception for your boss. I told him the African proverb from my curriculum: *Le grain de maïs ne dispute pas avec le poulet*; the kernel of corn doesn't argue with the chicken. He could not identify with a kernel of corn; he began a pattern of one short-term job after the other.

Once I was in his corner, I wanted to remediate the wrongs that had been done to him. Although he had not lived with his mother since he was a small child, he called her from time to time and tried to stay in touch. When Paul was born, he phoned to tell her he wanted her to see her grandson. She said that she had to go to bingo.

All week, Tammy spent her days home alone with Paul. He was her therapist, father confessor, best friend, and co-conspirator. She poured out her soul to him as he drank his bottle or lay on the changing table, his little bobble head nodding assent. When he was a year old, I suggested that we take a vacation to Florida. Tammy was a dutiful and loving mother, but I worried about what would happen when Paul became a headstrong toddler. What if she went off into one of her episodes of extreme regression, where she would veer towards tantrums and silent sulking pouts, and stalk off and disappear? What if she took leave of her senses when she was home alone with Paul? Floyd was beginning to see the challenges she posed. Sometimes when I came over on Fridays, he would wait until Tammy was out of earshot and then shake his head and say, "I can't even tell you."

So I hatched the plan to retire a couple of years early, buy a house in Florida where we could all four live, and try to insure that Paul would have enough love and nurturing to break the cycle. Spring vacation we drove to Fort Myers. While my parents were alive, we had gone there every Christmas and Easter. My grandfather grew up there and used to go back every winter, spending the rest of the year with us in New Jersey. When he was in Florida he sent postcards to my brother and me every day. My brother had recently found one addressed to me. It said, "Dear Margie, I'll tell the world." Although he died when I was five, I immediately understood the reference. A song named *Margie* was popular back in the early 40's. He gave me the record, and we played it on our wind-up Victrola. The whole sentence was, "I'll tell the world I love you." If someone should rework the song with "Paulie" instead of "Margie," then he would hear the refrain over and over: "After all is said and done, There is really only one. Paulie, Paulie, it's you."

19

MOVING TO FLORIDA

While the family of three enjoyed the pool and beach, I looked for a house. I told an old friend of my parents that I wanted three bedrooms—two on one side and one on the other. "Why that sounds like Ramon's house," she said. The next thing I knew, I was buying Ramon's house.

By summer of '02, I had closed on the house in Cape Coral, the town across the Caloosahatchee River from Fort Myers, and informed the school that this would be my last year. I had worked at Friends Seminary since I was twenty-nine. It was through the prism of this Quakerly institution that I saw the turmoil and political change spanning the years from 1969-2003. It was here that I watched generations of students mature from their first brush with French in fifth grade to eventual AP French. This school gave me the freedom to develop curricula, arrange exchanges with France and Guadeloupe, and lead groups to Quebec. It had been a nurturing matrix for me as much as for the students. The Community Church of New York was the other locus of my "neighborhood" within the impersonal city. With school and church, I had a comfortable niche. In retrospect, I wonder why I wasn't ill, looking into the abyss ahead. I would have to reinvent myself or at the very least reintroduce myself. But I was excited.

When I was young, I thought of retirement as the anteroom to death. I supposed it would be nice to have all that time, but I would probably be too decrepit and too terrified of curtain fall to get much out of it. In 1958, I played Cornelia Otis Skinner in *Our Hearts were Young and Gay*, back when gay meant nothing more than light-hearted. The big moment of my high school career was a monologue in which Cornelia takes a depressed look ahead at the life she thinks she is likely to live.

Like Shakespeare's melancholy Jacques, she outlines the sorry phases of life and ends by saying, "And then we'll be old, rocking on our porch, and I'll say to you (*fake tears are brewing*), 'Yes, George. Yes, George. It's been wonderful." Loud sobbing and thunderous applause from the audience. I was a triumph. I had conveyed the brevity and meaninglessness of life. I had especially communicated the pitifulness of old-age and retirement.

Life, as imparted by a seventeen-year-old, is pretty much a tale told by an idiot, but of course, I was just acting. Still, I bought the message, grateful that the rocking chair days were eons and eons away. But now here I was, minus a rocking chair. The rocker I bought to lull little Tammy to sleep was lost in the move.

Old age turns us into Buddhists; we live in the present. Those twenty years we normally think we have for plans shrink to ten, then five. I think of a dream I had many years ago when a teacher was retiring after fifty –yes fifty—years teaching at Friends Seminary. Dr. Hunter had never been absent in all that time except once when he had to have rabies shots after a weasel bit him as he protected his chickens on his New Jersey farm. I dreamed I saw him hit by a bus on Third Avenue. After my first feeling of distress, I thought, oh well, he's so old. Then I saw he was only knocked down. He was okay. In my dream, I experienced a powerful feeling of relief. I was just as relieved as I would have been if he were a young man just starting out. I got it. While you're alive, you're just as alive as anyone. Duh.

At the end of June of '03, we left Manhattan and Queens for good and headed down I-95 to our new home, where I would have to change my religion from four seasons to two. The old Toyota was like menopause. You froze or you roasted.

Paul was ensconced in his car seat between Tammy and Floyd in the back. Two cat carriers occupied the passenger seat in the front, stacked one on top of the other. Lucky, a stray they adopted, and Tinacat had never met but now communicated with catfight yowls for a thousand miles. I drove, spelled occasionally by Floyd, whom I'd taught to drive that year.

I suppose it comes as no surprise that I didn't think they should get a cat. I thought they shouldn't get married and shouldn't have a baby. This time I rotated my familiar 180 when Paul uttered his first word. About the time of his first birthday, Paul watched Lucky stroll by his high chair. He beat his hands excitedly against the tray and shouted, "Keecat!" Now the keecat was moving to Florida.

As we threaded our way to the Holland Tunnel, Paul called out a less comprehensible phrase. "Dooooeee yon!" Mile after mile of "Dooooee yon!" as he played with his little plastic Buzz Lightyear. After we finally cleared the tunnel, the tricky lane changes, and the gnarled traffic of the northeast, it occurred to me to ask, "Does anyone know what doooeee yon means?" His parents knew. With perfect synchronicity, they sang out, "To infinity and beyond!"

—So, Tammy, how did you feel about moving to Florida?

—Wuh hoo! You asked. I was very very happy - my home state plus I didn't have to freeze my butt off any more. That's a big wahoo. I would actually have help raising my kid because Floyd wasn't really participating in that. He was too bothered sleeping during the day and the morning and hanging out with his friends at night.

Before we left New York, Floyd worked at a Target in Queens. They liked him and saw to it that he would have a job awaiting at the Target in Cape Coral. He could even wear his same red shirt. The new hours were not to his liking, and I had to get up at 4:30 to insure he got there on time. I also had to drive him and pick him up in our only car. The lack of public transportation was a shock to all our systems, but even without subways, we rapidly adjusted to our new home. Paul enjoyed exploring the cupboards, so Floyd put locks on everything in the kitchen, including the refrigerator. The cats sniffed each other and entered into a wary truce. We loved our yard, abundant in mangoes, avocados, honey bell oranges, and pink grapefruits. The hibiscus and palms were a welcome and exotic change from the paved habitat we were used to. Whenever things look this good, I want to say "What could go wrong?" I need to be stopped because the answer is always, "Plenty."

20

APPLEBEE'S

Soon I got work teaching night courses in English Composition three times a week at a for-profit college, and later in the fall, the UU church I joined hired me as the Director of Religious Education. Tammy, who was dealing constantly with Paul, was getting increasingly glum. The helpless infant had learned to walk and to say a few words, most prominently "no." He was asserting his independence, and Tammy took it personally, as though she were receiving criticism from a vindictive peer. For much of the day he was her enemy. She lost all interest in bathing and began to smell. I found a course for her in jewelry making at a local art center and worried that her odor would further isolate her. Tammy and Floyd would often fight, and then she would stalk off, scaring both Floyd and me. I looked in the Yellow Pages for a therapist and found one we should all have been able to like.

My first thought was that Tammy and Floyd should go for marriage counseling. If fifty percent of marriages end in divorce, what were the odds for a couple with such a troubled history? Floyd refused. ("Shrinks mess with your mind.") He said that if Tammy had anything she needed to discuss, he was available.

So a morose and despondent Tammy went with me to see Mark. He saw depression and immediately referred Tammy to a psychiatrist, who re-diagnosed her as bipolar and prescribed several psychotropic drugs such as Lithium and Risperdal. Tammy's mood lightened immediately, and Floyd said, "I thank God for the meds."

Floyd helped with handyman jobs around the house. One end of our porch had storage with deteriorating hinges and knobs. Floyd, with Tammy's help, took down all the doors and painted them, installed new hinges, and added fasteners. For their trouble, I took the family to Sea World. We ate with Shamu, and that mischievous whale slapped the water with his tail as he swam by, soaking Paulie and me and our mac and cheese. Paul squealed with delight and clapped.

—-Tammy, what do you remember about the Applebee's incident?

—Don't remind me. My kid Paul was like misbehaving and crying and screaming and we were waiting for the food and the food was taking forever. I think we paid the bill. We got up. I placed him down on the ground and he was standing upwise and I grabbed his little hand because he was very young—he was one and a half or two something like that – I grabbed his hand like any other parent would. I was leading him toward the door to leave the Applebees. All of a sudden I feel my arm just go straight down; he decides to sit down and not move. He's still going *waa waa waa*. I was trying to pick him up and get him out of the restaurant and some lady in her own little booth or chair or whatever decided to call social services on me saying I was abusing him when I wasn't.

(Her dog, Princess barks.)

—Tell me about it, Princess. I agree. Have you ever seen me abuse that kid? I wish. There's times I wanted to but I don't. There's times when I've wanted to but I never have. I don't. Ask Charlotte she'll even tell you. She thought I was going to kill him right in front of her. But I said no there's a damn law against it damn it. She laughed too. She thought it was hysterical. The only person not laughing was Paul.

Welcome to Rashomon. Here's how I remember it. After church one Sunday, Tammy and I decided to have lunch at Applebee's. Paul, now almost three, should have been hungry, but instead he fussed and wouldn't stop struggling to get free to run around this very crowded restaurant.

"I'll take him out and walk around for a while. Maybe he'll settle down," I told her. "Order him a hotdog – and for me a burger,"

Outside, Paul struggled to pull away, a dangerous move since we were on Route 41, the busiest traffic artery of Fort Myers. Tammy and I had taken a course called Redirecting Your Child's Behavior. He would not be redirected. "Paulie, aren't you hungry? Mommy's getting you a hotdog. Yum," I crooned hopefully. He paused momentarily but then flailed his free hand and yanked the one I was holding him by.

Still stronger than he, I managed to pick him up. "Come on Paulie, let's take a deep breath. Oh, look at the flowers. What color are they? Do you like red? I'm getting hungry. We're going to eat and then we'll go home and see Daddy." He finally yielded to my patter. When he was calm for what seemed a reasonable time, I brought him back in.

The food had arrived, but once again Paul opted for freedom over sustenance. He pulled away, tripping a waitress carrying a full tray, and took off running.

"Tammy, you catch him. I'll pay up. Meet you at the car," I said.

Tammy ran after him and scooped him up, while I tried to get the check. There was a sizable noontime crowd around the door. Paul arched his back with all his strength as Tammy struggled to hold him. I paid for the uneaten food as fast as I could and then waited helplessly for the busy waitress to return with my credit card.

The knot of people blocked Tammy from a quick exit. Paul writhed and wriggled. People began to make suggestions. The confluence of criticism, obstinate child, hunger, and PDD swept Tammy into a maelstrom of misery. The din of chatter, clanking dishes and canned music, drowned out any words, but Tammy said something to her squirming offspring that resulted in horrified looks by the other patrons. She could have said "ass-hole" or "cut it out you little bastard." I didn't hear this time, but I had before. As I retrieved my card and rushed to the exit, someone uttered, "Child abuse." Others called on the management to take charge of the situation.

Tammy managed to get out of the place, muttering loudly about how people should leave her alone and yelling at Paul, who was now laughing from all the attention. She plopped him into his car seat with two Applebee's employees in hot pursuit, each proffering sweets to the adorable boy of the deranged mother. I came panting behind finishing in last place.

Tammy stormed away trailing a dark cloud just as I reached the car.

"Oh my God, she just left him here," said the taller one, whom I took to be the manager.

"That's because she saw I was here," I said. "She would never just leave him here. Don't worry. I'm the grandma. Thank you so much for all your help. His mom is upset. We'll take care of it. Thanks for your concern. We're okay," and I buckled Paul in and drove off hoping that I would find her.

I caught up with her as she crossed a little bridge out of the parking lot toward the very busy Cypress Lake Parkway. "Get in, Honey. Come on. You need to get in the car."

She pulled herself out of the black hole long enough to get in the car and say, "They think I'm a bad mother. What was I supposed to do? He was fighting me. I couldn't get out."

She slumped back into silence.

A few days later, she had still not recovered from this drama. I said, "Let's go to the movies." We left Paul with Floyd. The film was winding down when in they walked.

"What the??" said Tammy.

"Wait till you hear!" said Floyd. "We had a visitor." A lady from the Department of Children and Families had come by, following up on a call from the Applebee's people, who had noted my license plate number.

"Those meddling bitches," I said. "Not enough that they give sugar to an out-of-control child."

Floyd had turned on the charm, and he thought the worker saw that Paul was a well-tended child in a reasonable home. "Oh yeah. I was good." By a stroke of luck we had tidied up that day.

But there was more. While HRS, the parent agency to DCF, had waited ten months to do the paper work so that I could get little Tammy—and then only with the intervention of the President of the United States—and had also waited seven years to terminate parental rights so that I could adopt her, now times had changed; now DCF was Johnny-on-the-Spot. Tammy and I received a summons to appear at the DCF office in downtown Fort Myers.

A caseworker spoke with each of us separately. She told me that as long as I was in the picture, they wouldn't be concerned, but that something about Tammy and her behavior would go into a record.

I protested. "Tammy did the very best she could. Instead of helping her get a better purchase on the child, they accused her of abuse and gave the boy candy, which, believe me, he didn't need at that point."

She nodded agreement, but insisted, "Yes, but I can't take a chance in case later something bad happens to Paul."

21

FLOYD

Friendly and gregarious, Floyd immediately made new friends and spent evenings out partying, often returning late, after everyone else was asleep. He tried to include Tammy and brought her along several times. Though she attempted passable civility, she found herself at a loss to enter into conversation with these new people. Floyd complained to me that people were nice to her, but she clammed up.

He loved being a dad. The most cherished moments of his life were when baby Paul fell asleep in his arms. He required Paul to say "thank you" long before I thought it possible. He taught him to respond to "How much does Daddy love you?" by opening his arms wide and saying, "This much." When Floyd puttered about the house, he always had a sidekick. "You're a lucky man," I said. "You'll always have a best friend."

Once at the dinner table the topic of homosexuality came up. Floyd said, "I admit it, I tried it. "

"Well, many kids experiment," I said dismissively as I made sure the veggies got around.

But to Mark, the therapist, I said, "What is the matter with me? Why didn't I ask if he meant in the distant past or now?" I cursed my kneejerk liberalism. I should have gotten to the bottom of this. Could this explain why he left his wife and child every night to meet with friends I'd never met? But I minded my own business. He loved Tammy and Paul.

New fights with a manager: Floyd lost his job at Target. I thought of another African proverb: *l'escargot se déplace avec sa coquille*; the snail takes his shell with him. Floyd came with baggage and plenty of it. Still,, he found another job almost immediately at a nearby Publix.

I bought a car and gave him the old Toyota which was rapidly falling apart. He had to have wheels, so I gave him enough money for a down payment on a replacement.

"She disrespected me," he said of his manager when he lost the job at Publix. This time he did not bounce back so fast. He spent his time at his computer. By the time he got a job at UPS loading trucks, the Toyota was kaput. At the used car lot, he confessed that the down payment money was gone, frittered away in his evening rambles. He had no credit; I had to take responsibility for payments to make the deal.

Once when Floyd got home late, I was still up and asked if he could fix the VCR. Startled by the strong smell of marijuana, I later lay awake, wondering if this were the tip of the iceberg. I hadn't really considered addiction problems before because he was able to rouse himself and put in a day of work. I also figured that his nightly meanders were a way to avoid the pain of a wife whose tantrums were reminiscent of Rumpelstilskin when his name was exposed.

Tammy was left on her own most of the time. Every night, Paul fell asleep by her side. Floyd would come home to a wife and child in the bed.

Both Tammy and Floyd were smoking cigarettes, but followed the rule and kept it outside. In retrospect marijuana seems trivial, but I had said, "No drugs." I discovered that I could buy a kit at the drugstore, test his urine and find out for sure what he was taking. I bought one.

When Floyd came in from UPS, I told him that I had smelled marijuana on him and that I couldn't have drug use. I told him that he knew that. He said, "You don't trust me."

"I trust you," I said, "but I trust my nose more."

I showed him the kit I had bought. "If you want to change my mind here's a cup you can pee in." It would be an understatement to say that he flew into a rage. I said it was pee in a cup or move out. He said that he would not leave, and he most certainly would not pee in a cup. I called 911. Before the police arrived, he had already left. Tammy told me later that he was hiding across the street laughing. The cops told me that I could not throw him out, that he had rights, and that I had to give him notice. They said I could post it on the garage door. I wrote a note saying that I was giving him notice to move out, but that I would change my mind on two conditions: if Tammy wanted him back, and if he would agree not to use drugs.

I thought Tammy would resist and demand that he come back. He visited her and Paul several times when I was out, and they seemed to be getting along. Friends of mine who regularly smoked weed thought I was absurd. I considered softening my stand. But Tammy surprised me. She said that she wanted a divorce. She was feeling neglected and lonely. She thanked me. She said she wanted out but didn't know how.

A friend of Floyd's came by to trim our shrubs and said that Floyd had tried to crash at his place, but he wouldn't let him. He said Floyd was living in the car, had no place to shower, and was fired by UPS for smelling bad.

—What happened to your marriage?

—I was in a marriage by myself. He sleeps all day and hangs out with his teenage friends at night. I don't need that. I was left alone to take care of the clothing, the house work and the kid and making dinner. So much for one person.

Tammy maintained some contact with him and knew that he had a job in Fort Myers at a 7-Eleven. A couple with dubious intentions let him sleep on the couch in their trailer. One night Floyd came back and knocked on my window. I found him in the driveway, near tears. He had been in a fight with the couple over money, and the guy took a baseball bat to the car. The windshield was cracked.

There stood this beautiful, disheveled, street-smart young guy, so lost and alone. I had the hopeless feeling that it was too late. His horrific childhood weighed him down. The incarceration and homelessness that marked his early adulthood would keep cycling back. This was the legacy of foster care and the foster care system. If you don't have a mother or father who loves you enough to raise you, and no one comes along to adopt you, then you emerge into adulthood with Mount Everest in front of you. Floyd had a mother who would rather play bingo than meet her grandson.

Floyd had no place to go. For four years he had been my boy. I let myself be the only mother who ever loved him. If only I were rich, I'd rent a place for him where he could co-parent his child. Though I was the one who threw him out, I still wanted to pull him back in.

But Tammy had been to Legal Aid. The divorce was in the works. I couldn't very well invite him in without a plan to invite him out on her behalf. I told him to sleep in the car. If he wanted to go back to New York, I would pay his way. I reminded him that the car was mine and someday I would want it back for Tammy.

He found another place and kept his job at 7-Eleven. This time he roomed with a father and son, and they expected rent. I continued to pay the insurance and payments on the dilapidated Ford Escort.. Feeling like a monster, I cashed my last certificate of inherited stock and paid off the balance on the car, figuring that if I owned it outright, I could get it back more easily. My plan was to teach Tammy to drive and then give her the car. I enlisted the help of my friend Nona.. She drove me to the 7-Eleven. I planned to drive home in the car.

Floyd spotted me from behind the counter. I saw him steady himself. The knot of a huge tension headache rendered me almost powerless. "I've come for the car," I managed.

"Oh, sure. But not right now."

"Oh."

"Not good enough," chimed in Nona. "Give Marge the keys."

I held up the title as Nona called 911. The police came and insisted Floyd give me the keys. I drove the car home, pounding head, cracked windshield and all.

That was his last day at 7-Eleven. He had no way to get to work. I don't know how he got home that night. He used the monitor and then the other parts of the computer I had given him to stay afloat financially. When nothing was left to barter, his landlord made him leave. Using a library computer, he emailed asking if the offer to pay his way to New York was still good. I emailed back, "Of course." He walked the distance from the library.

He felt he had no way to keep going in Florida. He said he had tried to sleep on a park bench, but was roused by the police. He felt that he knew his way around the services in New York and would do all right there. I got him an airline ticket for the next day and said he could sleep on the couch.

Paul dreamed of going in our new pool with daddy and it happened. I took pictures as I watched them play – the same chubby cheeks, the same warm, ingratiating smile. I thought that this was a bond that could not be broken. I went inside and found a letter addressed to Paul. Rambling and depressed, it cautioned Paul, "Don't become a loser like me." But hope had not completely died. When we came back from the airport, the letter was nowhere to be found.

I stayed in touch with Floyd. He continued to use libraries to contact me via email. I let him know his divorce went through. I told him Paul missed him and would like to see him. For thirty years I had gone to see a group of old friends in Brooklyn for New Year's Eve. This time I brought Tammy and Paul. We stayed in a B and B on 35th St. owned by our old church. We had our own little walk-up apartment.

Floyd looked strained and defeated when we met him at a McDonald's on 25th Street. He tried to muster some of his old cheer for Paul's sake. By night he slept on the subway, and by day he begged on the street. While I was catching up with old friends, the three of them went to the ice skating rink at Chelsea Piers and the movies and hung out at the apartment. Tammy said that when he took his shoes off, you couldn't breathe in the room. In his condition, he hadn't a prayer of getting a job. I told him I would pay for two nights in a motel for him to get cleaned up and look for a job. I'm sure the funds were redirected.

The thought of Floyd unable to lie down in a warm place, of Floyd shuffling about in the cold in such worn shoes that only castoff cardboard protected him from the icy pavement, of Floyd being roused from a temporary repose on the subway tormented my sleep. Finally he emailed me that Mayor Bloomberg was embarrassed by all the bums lying in the gutters and had made available some city-owned buildings for permanent housing. Floyd got an efficiency on 24th Street. I thanked a God I don't believe in.

22

A BREAK

—Tammy, do you remember that time when Paul called 911?

—You mean against me. I wanted to kill him then too.

It started when I picked up Anne, my old teaching chum from Friends Seminary at the airport. She had come from New York to attend a Master Naturalist conference with me at a bucolic center in Haines City, a two-and-a-half-hour ride from here. As soon as we got home, her British roots kicked in, and she had "a nice cup of tea." She was asleep on the porch, and I was beginning to doze when Tammy came in and said, "Paul's not doing too good."

"What's wrong?"

"He can't breathe too good."

"Okay, Honey, I'll take a look. "

Paul, now six, was sitting on Tammy's bed, coughing continuously. The thick smell of Vicks Vaporub was in the air. He tried to get relief from his inhaler, but to no avail. Next to him was a pot from the kitchen. "In case I throw up," he gasped between coughs.

"Tammy, he needs to get to the hospital. Let's get in the car. "

Fortunately, respiratory problems are a priority in ERs, right up there with bleeding. He was whisked into a bed immediately and given oxygen and a shot. Tammy and I gazed down at him helplessly. The doctor came in and asked if he had thrown up.

"No," he said, "but I got a pot from the kitchen just in case."

"Just in case," said the doctor. "Smart boy."

The hospital was air-conditioned beyond endurance. Tammy and I shivered in the icy, antiseptic air while the personnel hurried about, checking a device that gently pinched his finger, indicating his level of oxygen. It didn't rise fast enough. We waited and froze. I said to a nurse, "Maybe you don't notice because you're working so hard, but it's freezing in here."

"Oh, believe me, we notice." She handed each of us a heated blanket.

For two hours, we stood, wrapped like squaws, watching our sweet boy struggle under a harsh fluorescent glare. The sporadic emergency pages and beeping heart monitors furnished the background noise for my thoughts of Warner. Paul looked white, but thank God he didn't look blue. Slowly his breathing improved. A last check of his oxygen indicated that he was good to go. It was 3:30 AM.

Maybe what came next wouldn't have happened if it weren't for the exhaustion of that night.

Anne had been totally oblivious to our absence. "Is he okay now?" she asked over her morning tea and porridge.

"He's fine. This happens to him sometimes – but never this bad—when he has congestion from a cold. Now he'll be fine. "

Late in the morning Tammy roused herself. I thought she had been perfect at the hospital. No different from any concerned parent. But now she was gloomy and brimming with irritation. Paul continued to sleep. "You remember Anne and I are going to the Master Naturalist thing for the weekend."

"Yeah, sure." said Tammy with that dull woe-is-me voice that signaled trouble brewing.

"You have enough money, right? I left you food, right?"

"Right." Her face was sullen. If she was trying to make me feel selfish, she was succeeding. I knew that leaving her alone would be taking a chance. Anne had come from New York for this conference. We had been planning it for months. "Tammy, I'm sorry to leave you, but Paul is okay now. If anything happens call 911."

"Go ahead. Who asked you to stay? Have fun," she said. "My life sucks. It's beginning to suck more and more every day."

"You were great at the hospital," I said. "You'll do a great job. We'll be back on Sunday."

With misgivings, we took off for Haines City in the afternoon, leaving a grumbling Tammy and a cheery Paul behind.

The center was on a lake. Spanish moss hung from the abundant live oaks that dipped their branches toward the water. After settling in our room, we listened to a presentation on light pollution. I could scarcely muster outrage at the disturbance to ecosystems, preoccupied as I was about Tammy and Paul.

As soon as the talk ended, I called home. When a man answered., I thought I had a wrong number. He said he was a police officer. He said that six-year-old Paul called 911 because mommy was "acting funny." When they got there she was sitting on the floor mumbling something about never getting a break. The officer wanted to know where he could take Paul because he couldn't leave him with Tammy. Two houses away from us lived a couple who had gone to college with my brother. He said they would take him there.

"I'm sorry, Anne. I have to go home. Should I leave you here?"

"No. Marge, I'll come with you. Don't worry about it. "

We started out the long lane through the woods. It definitely had no light pollution. Only my headlights revealed the dirt trail. Suddenly a raccoon dashed in front of me. I hit it hard.

"Oh, what should I do?"

Anne, the consummate lover of animals, said, "You have to forget about it. Just get home. You can only worry about so much."

Highway 17 was deserted at this hour. I noticed signs to unfamiliar places —Frostproof and Bartow. Tammy thought she could never get a break? I was the one who could never get a break. I couldn't even go away for a weekend with a friend. My child remained a child even though she was almost thirty.

Anne settled down to a nap. A nagging feeling of bitter regret pushed away my worry over how Tammy and Paul were doing. I was stuck with Tammy. Nothing I did could make this nestling fledge. And Annie had come all this way for a weekend that wasn't to be.

The road led south and a little west through central Florida between the two teeming coasts, below the populated Interstate 4 corridor. I passed one gas station, on this lonely trek, a bright oasis in the gloom. The lottery sign made me wish I had a mil. If I put it in the tax-free municipal bond fund at Valueline or Vanguard it could make four percent per year. No, probably three. Even so, that would be thirty thousand a year. If I lived for ten more years and never used it, it could be about a million four hundred thousand. That could provide Tammy an income of more than forty thousand a year.

Just wishing. And doing arithmetic.

The two-lane road opened up to four lanes for a brief moment. I got an odd child., I thought. I would have her forever. I thought of Sisyphus, condemned to push a rock to the top of a hill every day. Over and over. Yet in Camus' telling of the story, as Sisyphus strides down the hill, we should imagine him happy. I had much more reason than Sisyphus to feel happy. Could he love his rock as much as I loved Tammy? I was driving down a deserted road in the middle of nowhere. Cows were undoubtedly sleeping with their ibises in the dark fields. A friend was sleeping on my right. I guess I was striding back down, because I felt happy.

Tammy was awake when we got in. "I miss him," she cried plaintively. "I don't know where he is."

"He's with Jean and Mike. I'm sure he's asleep. We'll get him tomorrow. "

The next morning I walked up the street and found him chatting with Jean. As we walked back home, I asked Paul why he'd called the police. "I wanted them to tell Mommy the rules," he said.

"Tell Mommy the rules," I said. I leaned over and kissed the top of his head. "Smart boy."

PART V

2007- PRESENT

23

EXPANDING THE FAMILY

"Grandma, some guy is going to ask Mom out." Paul said, running into the kitchen.

"Huh?" I said as I pulled the meat off a rotisserie chicken for a noodle casserole.

"His name is Mario* and he knows her from when Dad was here."

"Layla!" As usual, the hound was underfoot hoping for a moment of inattention. "Okay. Why do you think he's going to ask Mom out?

"He said he liked her and asked if she was going out with anyone. I gave him her cell and told him he should call her."

"Well, aren't you the matchmaker!"

"Oh yeah. This will make Mom very happy."

Mario did ask Tammy out over and over, but I hadn't met him. It seemed to me that he was avoiding Tammy's family, both Paul and me.

Tammy got a call on her cell. "What's going on, Tammy?"

"I'm going to hang out with Mario."

"Why don't you invite him over? I haven't met him, you know. Now where are you going?"

"To take a shower. He said, 'Take a shower and come over.' He said he would pick me up."

I was standing in the driveway when he came by. He pulled up in an old Camaro, which evidently had no muffler. Amid the *vroom vrooms*, he opened his window and said, "Hello."

Tammy ran out into the drive and jumped into the car. Off they went, the din of the engine telegraphing his presence to everyone in the neighborhood.

What I had seen was a round head topped with curly black hair. I was struck by how spherical his head was. That was all I saw.

The next day he came by again, but this time he came in. I once again thought of a sphere, but this applied to his whole being. If I were to draw him, it would be the way you draw a snowman, except that the bottom circle would be two short legs. He was decked out in bling – rings on four fingers and a chunky gold necklace.

"Hi Mario. I'm so glad to meet you. Tammy really has enjoyed knowing you. Here. Have a seat."

"Hi, yeah, I would have come over sooner but I'm so busy. My grams has so many appointments."

"Oh, that's okay."

"Yeah, I'm really happy to know Tammy. Thank goodness she dumped that awful husband. Oh yeah, I met her then and I thought what a loser and Tam's such a sweet kid. For once someone who likes me for me. Most chicks get wind that my family has money and that's all they care about. Not Tammy. The least materialistic person I've met."

"You're right. She doesn't care much about things. So what do you do, Mario. I think she said you were in construction."

"Construction, yes. But I'm more a car mechanic. Right now I'm waiting for disability to kick in—- had an accident with a ladder on a job. But mostly I love cars. That's another thing. So does Tam. She's been helping me put together a Lexus my dad gave me. But I can do most things – fix things, build things, oh, yeah."

"That's wonderful. Is your dad around here?"

"He goes back and forth between Naples and Connecticut. He came over from Italy when he was a kid and worked as a butcher at the A&P. This is some story. You won't believe this. A lady who bought meat from him asked him to help her sell her house. So he tried his hand at Real Estate. First time out of the gate, he made 50,000 bucks. That was the end of the A&P. I guarantee you that."

One evening he joined Paul, some neighborhood kids, and me when we walked our hound, Layla. He said he was taking care of his grandmother because he had promised his grandfather she would stay in the house and never go to a nursing home. I said, "Really, Mario, you are a stand-up guy to do that."

He said, "I can't believe you're saying that."

"What do you mean?"

"Well generally I don't have much of a track record with mothers-in-law. "

When Christmas came around he assembled the trampoline I'd bought for Paul. Tree rats got into out attic and he screened off vents to block their passage.

After he saw Tammy's room, which looked like an episode of Hoarders, he said, "I don't know. This could be a deal breaker."

But he stuck with her and encouraged her to try once again to do some modeling. In high school she had taken a course at the Barbizon School in New York, but nothing had come of it except for one day of glamourous triumph when she arrived at school in her professionally applied make-up looking gorgeous. Now she found a little school in the neighborhood and once again began to assemble some photos. Before long she was doing a runway event at a mall.

I found myself with time on my hands. Paul was in day camp and Tammy was spending more and more time with Mario, helping him with Grams by taking her to appointments in the mornings when Mario wasn't up.

There was a widower at church who I imagined was lonely. It seemed to me that he made a point of chatting with me during coffee hour. He always wore guayaberas and had a cute dimply smile. I heard him mention to someone that he had a blind date. *Let's not be stupid,* I thought. I sent him an email asking if he'd like to go to the movies. Bold as this was, I figured I was doing him a favor and that I might make a friend in the process. He left it to me to pick the movie. Nothing much was playing, so I chose a Sandra Bullock film, *The Proposal.* In retrospect, this seems a tad unsubtle.

What are the odds? Tammy and I both found ourselves in a relationship. Mario sent Don an email welcoming him to the family, to which neither of them yet belonged. Presumptuous, but I felt his heart was in the right place.

Don and I continued to see movies and eat out together. He had had a long career as a psychology professor. He loved history and had written a history of clinical psychology. After he retired, he went back to college to get a BA in history. At the point when we got involved, he was finishing up a masters, and I was teaching English comp at ITT Tech. So, we were just another young couple starting out, except for the forty extra years we had occupied the planet. He proposed to me in our favorite Asian restaurant. I choked on my sushi, and eventually got around to saying, "Will we love each other?"

It was too obvious. We went to buy a ring. So easy. Like breathing air.

When I told Tammy and Paul that we were getting married, Paul punched the air and said, "Yes!"

Everybody showed up for the wedding. Our set said, "It's nice to go to an event that isn't a funeral." Karen, Mary, Donna, Bob, Ariana, Ginny, John, Anita, Doyle – they came from far away. Tammy was my matron of honor, and Paul was the ring bearer. Paul at first refused, but capitulated when we agreed to buy him a tux. My brother walked me down the aisle. My new brother-in-law came from New Jersey to be Best Man. Don's daughter came from Kansas. We had written our vows, and promised to love each other as we were. We all sang a song with the lyric, "I'll give you hope, when hope is hard to find." A friend read, "Oh the places you'll go," by Dr. Seuss.

Don wore a white dinner jacket loaned to him by a neighbor. Her husband, of the same size, had died and left her with the suit. She said that she looked at his picture that morning and said, "Chuck, your suit is getting married again." I wore a white dress because, Hey, I'd never been married before. It's amazing what you get when you Google *older bride*.

Mario proved to be a big help. Marsha and Elissa, who had been students when I directed a year abroad program four decades earlier, were having car trouble. Mario gave the vehicle his professional once-over, and they were on the road again.

We spent the night in the lovely Indigo Hotel in downtown Fort Myers where haiku abounded. Then the next morning I went for a root canal. Yes, I went to my own wedding with a toothache. But I didn't even notice it. The dentist put me on amoxicillin, and off we went to catch the plane to New York.

I was happy. So many times I had thought, if you miss the boat when you're in your twenties, then you have missed it forever. Don seemed to me to be a miracle. He welcomed sharing the challenges Tammy and Paul entailed. He found Tammy more interesting than distressing. Having directed the clinical psychology program at the University of Miami for many years, he was well versed in the gamut of psychological disorders including PDD. He observed her and finally said, "I've never seen anything quite like it." His daughter had opted not to have kids, so he was happy to become Paul's grandpa.

He said that I was his soul mate. I told Anne about how interesting it was to hear him talk about his archival research, about how I admired his lively mind, still tackling new disciplines. She said, "At last, Marge, you have found someone you can respect."

I loved showing Don my old haunts; the Morgan Library, the Community Church, where both Tammy and Paul had had Naming and Dedication Ceremonies, my school, and my old office space. He had never before been to the Metropolitan Museum or the Frick. I got to see old wonders with new eyes. That was our honeymoon; then we went on a trip.

We rented a car and picked up Paul at the Westchester airport. Tammy and Mario passed Paul off to us and went to his family in Connecticut while Don, Paul, and I went to Lake George, to meet up with my New Year's Eve friends. John grilled burgers as we all sat on their front deck, overlooking the lake. For years, this had been a place of happy times. Donna, Bob, Mary, and Ariana were there, sipping white wine. Paul was in his glory tagging along after the two pretty teenage girls in the party. Don slipped into the group as though he had always been there. I noticed that when he told his daughter about the lake, he said *"our* old friends."

For the last phase of our trip, we went to visit my brother and family in the Poconos. As we drove down the highway, Don sang Woody Guthrie's "Let's go riding in the car, car, Let's go riding in the car car." I applauded; Paul said, "That's supposed to be good?"

We passed Paul off to Tammy and Mario in New Paltz, and I broke out with the worst case of hives in history. My sister-in-law, a nurse, said it looked like an allergic reaction and to take Benadryl. She quickly suspected that the amoxicillin from the dentist was the culprit. The hives got worse. She said, "You need a shot of Prednisone. Go to the hospital."

I got relief almost immediately from the shot. We went on to LaGuardia to catch the plane home.

"Identification," said the baggage handler.

Don quickly produced his, but I went through my purse over and over. I quickly realized that I had been so befuddled at the hospital that I had lost my driver's license in the process of showing my insurance cards.

"This is a real problem. No ID. Don't know what I can do," said the airport man, shaking his head. "Very bad."

Don slipped him a twenty.

"Follow me." We paraded after him through the impossibly crowded airport, stopping momentarily along the way as he conversed in Spanish with uniformed colleagues. We got to the gate and embarked directly! Who knew? —A twenty did the trick!

24

BOYFRIEND FROM HELL

One Saturday afternoon, Don and I took Paul and his friend Brian to the movies. After the show, we were supposed to deliver the boys to Tammy and Mario. The film let out a little earlier than expected so since we were in the car, Don thought he might as well take them directly over to Mario's. I felt distinct trepidation as we pulled into Mario's driveway. I had picked up a quality of inflexibility in him. We had left it that we would call Tammy when we got out of the movies. I felt we were crossing a line.

"Maybe we should wait."

"Oh well, we're here."

Don went up to the door and rang the bell. It didn't seem to work, so he knocked. Nobody came to the door so we went home.

I *am* Madame Claire Voyante. I felt something bad would happen if we didn't go strictly by plan. Mario emailed us excoriating Don for "knocking obnoxiously" on his door. He made wild accusations about leaving the kids in the hot sun, called us white trash, and chewed out my mild-mannered professor for "raising your voice continuously" to Tammy, whom he had renamed Tami.

Despite the nastiness of the email, Don suggested a family meeting. But the hostilities had advanced too far on Mario's part for him to want harmony in any way. Neither Don nor I had ever encountered this level of vitriol. We got another email where my name had become the Farm Animal and Don was referred to as The Walking Corpse. We were in our first year of marriage, and I felt guilty that I had brought Don into such a sorry situation. When he first proposed in the Asian restaurant, I had gone home and emailed him that he was a brave man.

"You didn't know how brave you'd have to be, did you?"

"Oh well, in for a penny, in for a pound," he said and kissed me.

"In for a penny, in for a ton, it would appear."

Tammy began sleeping at Mario's and leaving Paul with us. I took him to school every day and then Tammy picked him up and brought him back to our house. I walked around in a state of subdued melancholy. I felt that Tammy had sided with the enemy. I was too distressed to make excuses for her. This time, I felt my daughter had left her body and a hostile being had intruded into our family. Was there any moral center to her? Was there no limit to the abuse she would let Mario heap on Don and me? And more important, if Paul became the target, would she stand up for him?

Don's daughter, Lauri, came for Thanksgiving. Lauri was a great friend to the environment in and out of her job. She was a solid waste management supervisor at a landfill. Bold and beautiful with flowing honey hair, Lauri had the pragmatic chops to turn her idealism into action. The city council members of Lawrence, Kansas, quaked in their boots when Lauri came forward during private-citizen time to present her passionate and tightly reasoned arguments.

For the day after Thanksgiving, I got tickets for the Oxbow and Riverlore boat ride on the Caloosahatchee. I thought Lauri would enjoy hearing about how our river was straightened in the interests of commerce and how the oxbows, small elbows off the river, remained as parenthetical reminders of what used to be. Tammy didn't come for Thanksgiving and then didn't come to the boat ride. Any hope I had of creating a blended family was dashed. The family was split in two, with only Paul fully a member of each part.

Gradually Mario engineered a break between Don and me and Tammy and Paul. I was no longer permitted to drive Paul to school. Then Tammy took Paul and moved in with Mario. Still, Tammy and I remained in contact. She would stop in to have coffee with me after she dropped Paul off on days she thought Mario wouldn't notice. She was afraid to linger. He wouldn't like it.

"Honey, a relationship isn't supposed to be like jail."

"No, no. It's not like that. But he'll be up soon. I'd better get going."

A friend said that women in abusive relationships break up seven times before they finally manage to get out. Prophetic words!

We had offered to take Paul to the Unitarian camp in North Carolina. Tammy accepted and I signed him up. In June, Tammy came home, vowing to never see Mario again. All her possessions were deposited in our driveway.

A week later, she decided to go back to Mario.

She left Paul with me only to have Mario send the cops to pull him away while he was swimming in the pool. The police had no choice, but they saw the situation. One sternly told Mario to get in the car and let the boy say good-bye to his grandmother. "Don't worry," Mario called as they drove away. "He can still go to the camp with you. "

That was the first time he had spoken to me in nearly a year!

Privately, the officers said, "You're in a tough spot. Keep records."

Paul, Don, and I escaped for two weeks to the spectacular mountaintop. I believe that this trip gave us strength for what was to come.

During breakup number four, Mario emailed Tammy, claiming to have contacted SSI and DCF. "By the time they are done with you, your son will be GONE, your SSI, Cash Assistance, your Food stamps and whatever mind you have left, will be gone! YOUR LOSS! SEE YA!"

Still, she went back and took Paul with her.

When people at church asked Don what was wrong, he said. "The boy-friend from hell."

Don and I planned to dress as Shrek and Fiona for Halloween, a day that will live in family infamy. Breakup number five was well underway. Tammy left Mario, brought Paul home, and swore that she was done with Mario. He was a creep. She hated him. All her possessions arrived in big boxes.

During this stay, I decided to play hardball. I was an amateur, but I figured I hadn't much to lose. Tammy still had that white Ford Escort I had taken back from Floyd. I told her that she could keep it, and I would continue to pay the insurance on it if she let me see Paul once a week. She said, "Sure." After all she was never going to see Mario again. I put it in writing and we both signed. I put in the provision that if she didn't comply, she had to relinquish the car.

But then, on Halloween she went back.

She left a note explaining, "I have to follow my heart and my heart is with him. I might be dumb, stupid, or crazy, but I need to give this relationship one more chance."

A weeping Fiona, in the homeliest drab green dress I could find, I dumped the sweets into the plastic pumpkin. Don in a full-head Shrek mask, with those mushroom-trumpet ears, said, "Maybe we should turn out the lights and stay in."

"No," I sobbed. "Brave face, Shrek."

I checked my email one last time before I went out to greet the goblins in my driveway. "Go ahead and take the car. It's in the Wal-Mart parking lot. You're not seeing Paul."

Two miserable monsters handed out the chocolate, and I ate my share. Up the street I saw a familiar spaceman knock on a door. Before he could come to our driveway, Mario shoved him into his muffler-free Camaro and sped off.

Mario had damaged the Ford Escort beyond repair and the mechanic, who used to work with Mario, put on the receipt that the damage was "Vandalism by Mario." He and the tow truck operator thought I should call the police. I felt I would like to see Mario in jail, but I couldn't do it. I feared that anything I did would only further alienate Tammy and Paul.

So just like that, they were gone from my life and I had a piece of useless junk.

I had enrolled Paul in soccer. Like a desperate groupie, every week I went to watch the mid-week practice and then on Saturdays, the game. Tammy and Mario treated me as though I were invisible, but Paul shot me a little nod as he hustled down the field.

I missed them. I particularly missed Paul. He was a fifth grader, the developmental level I love the most. If there is anything in my life that overwhelms me with rancor, it is that I could not be there for Paul's fifth grade. Ten-year-olds are at the pinnacle of childhood. Still safe from the looming craziness of adolescence, they know virtually everything important that adults know. I would rather chat with a 10-year-old than with a teen, or an adult for that matter. They see reality more clearly and objectively, without the haze of ideological and political filters that distort our perceptions as we age. I felt robbed.

At night when I couldn't sleep, I would go into Tammy's room and hug her pillow. I worried. Isolating a person from her family was part of abuse. Mario wrote an email claiming an order of protection against us.

I took a course in mindfulness, and every day I practiced the loving kindness meditation. The soothing voice of the instructor on my CD said this was the antidote to anger and irritation. She advised me to bring to mind someone important to me. I thought of Tammy. I said out loud,

May you be well.

May you be happy.

May you abide in peace.

May you feel safe and secure.

May you feel loved and cared for.

Then I thought of Paul and said the words again, trying, as she suggested, to wrap him in the warmth of my caring.

She said to think of someone who had hurt me. I thought of Mario. But I could not say the words. Nirvana and Enlightenment would never be mine, I guess.

Soccer season was over and I had no further occasions for getting a glimpse of Paul. I Googled their names, longing for some meager sign of life. Then there they were on my computer screen in a news article that popped up. Paul had won the Do the Right Thing Award and was feted at city hall. As a fifth grader, the terminal elementary year, he was an official triple A safety patrol, helping the younger kids with parent pick-up. He memorized every child's car. Parent pick-up had never been so deftly administered.

There was Paul, displaying his certificate, with Tammy on one side and a uniformed officer on the other. I swelled with pride in absentia. Tammy's expression was blank. I wondered how she was doing. At the same time I was furious with her. She must have known how painfully excluded I would feel. Mario's control must have torn her, at least a little.

I sent Tammy and Paul money at Christmas and on their birthdays in February. For about four months, the checks went uncashed. This was a long stretch, and I fretted so much that Don suggested we see a lawyer. Maybe we had some rights. I got on the mailing list of an organization for alienated grandparents.

The lawyer, Larry, said we could sue for custody, but our chances were not good. Figuring that the dad had some say in where Paul should be, he got a private investigator in New York to approach Floyd to see if he would help me. I hoped he would feel I would be a better bet for Paul than the new male interloper. Floyd was indeed living on 24th Street, but he always ran the other way when he saw the detective coming, probably thinking this had something to do with the child support, which at that point he had never paid..

I wanted to go to court. No matter how bad the odds, I figured that I would win if I just got a chance to explain to the judge how much of a parent I had been to Paul since his birth.

As soon as Tammy was informed of the court date, "Tami" sent me an email that claimed to have a video of me "DRUNK with only one sock on, no shoes, in the rain, driving your car to get MORE alcohol. Even though we tried to steer the truck away so Paul wouldn't see your DRUNK DISGUSTING SELF, it was too late. He said, 'Isn't that Nana' we told him no but he already saw you stumble out of your car. (got that on film too, a great vision of an appropriate parental figure, huh). . . .see you in court if you have the stomach for it."

Well, I did have the stomach for it. I couldn't bear for Paul to be in that home another minute. Nona and Anne produced notarized letters extolling me as the height of sobriety, and a noted psychologist, who knew Don for decades testified, that he "always exhibited the highest standards of honesty and integrity."

In the courtroom, Larry greeted Tammy's lawyer, a youngish attractive woman in a dark pants suit, very professional, nice nails, long wavy hair pulled back in a tortoise shell clip. As they were exchanging pleasantries, Tammy came in, hiding under her hair. I knew that being adversarial with me was more than she could handle. She looked woozy, clutched the wall as though she were weak in the knees, and plopped down on the floor, legs straight out in front of her, looking overcome, perhaps with dizziness. Mario quickly stood her on her feet. I thought, she's so upset she's not eating. Mario would never think of sushi therapy.

Don and I sat with Larry in the first row of the visitors' gallery. Tammy's lawyer led an unsteady Tammy to the table in front of the judge. Like a confidant or intimate friend, the lawyer kept up a steady stream of comments, whispered into Tammy's ear. Tammy nodded repeatedly. Maybe she was gathering strength. I felt my divided loyalty. I wished I could help Tammy. I knew she would be plunged into extreme misery if she lost Paul. He was her most wonderful life achievement. It turned out that Tammy did take after me. Motherhood was central. We were two women caught in a classic agon; fighting her for Paul felt almost Greek.

The judge called us to order. I looked over at Mario, exuding smarmy confidence, at the other end of the row. It wasn't about Tammy. It wasn't from Tammy that I was trying to wrest Paul. It was from this man who had isolated them from their family, who had hatched revolting, demeaning lies to wield power over them.

Mario was not allowed to sit with her. He was not a party to the action in any legal way because they weren't married, and he wasn't Paul's stepfather. He wouldn't have a chance to fight dirty, to vilify us, and even if he did, I knew the truth of my position would be evident to anyone sane. He couldn't beat me. Passion, reason, and a slew of notarized letters from upstanding citizens were on my side.

Tammy's lawyer stood up and asked to be heard. "Your Honor, this case has no standing. The complainant did not house the minor child, Paul Martin, when the writ was filed. According to . . . " and then she cited some cockamamie statute that said we couldn't bring this action unless the child had been in our home the night before we submitted the complaint.

The judge mulled this statement. "Does the lawyer for the complainant have anything to say?"

Sheepishly, Larry said, "Your Honor, I was not aware of this statute."

"Well, then, case dismissed," and he pounded the gavel.

I turned to Larry, "What happened?"

"I'm really sorry," he said. "We've been thrown out on a technicality. Keep on working on Tammy. She's your weak link."

"My poor Paulie," I said to Don. So that was that.

Still, I thought it would filter to Paul that I loved him enough to try to get custody of him.

We looked over and saw Mario congratulating their counsel. Score one for the bad guys.

In May, I was sitting at my computer when Layla ran to the garage door barking wildly. There stood Paul, just as natural as if he had been coming and going every day.

Walking through the door he said, "Calm down, Layla! Yes, Daddy's here. Good girl. Yes, yes, Daddy's here. Are you my good dog?"

"Paul!" I cried. "Don, Paul's here. "

"Yup. I'm here for a visitation."

"Well, let me get a look at you! "

There he was, my boy, his mop of nearly black hair spilling into his eyes. Such a sturdy lad with such a confidant swagger. Broad shoulders, like his dad, but a pursed mouth like Tammy. Come to my arms my beamish boy. I must have been chortling.

I threw my arms around him. He put up with it more than he really wanted to – "Paul, Paul, my precious boy, so happy you're here"—and then he pulled away. "Where's Princess?"

Don came in from the living room. "Well, Paul! Great to see you!"

"Hi Grandpa. I'm doing a visitation. Yeah, this is the new thing. I'm going to be doing visitations."

"Suits us," I said.

Don squeezed my arm. "We've got our Paulie," I said. *Darling boy, if you knew how much I've missed you!* Here he was, by himself. I had been wondering if I was beating myself up with another case of unrequited love. But no. It was his idea to be here. He had driven them so crazy that they finally gave in.

Paul walked into the kitchen, turning around dishes and jars, checking the familiar against the newly changed.

"Grandpa, where's Princess?" he asked as he turned to caress Layla's ears.

A sharp bark answered his question. He went into the bedroom and roughhoused with the ecstatic dachshund. "Princess, don't be jealous. Daddy loves you, too." Princess rolled on her back, exulting in a tummy rub.

You would think I won the Nobel Peace Prize. I sent out a missive to all my friends.

> —Tammy, you don't know how terrible it was not seeing you and Paul all those months.
> —Terrible for you! I couldn't see you or talk to you. He cut off all my friends on Facebook. He wouldn't even let me communicate with my brothers.
> —Couldn't you have left him?
> (long pause)
> —I guess you've never been in an abusive relationship.

Spring turned to summer. Tammy and Paul came home again. It was the seventh time, so I was hopeful. Paul said that at Mario's he cried himself to sleep every night. He never wanted to go back there again. Paul and Brian were once again inseparable. Brian, too, had been banished from Paul's life, and the boys were happy to take up where they had left off.

Don was giving a paper in Montreal, and although Tammy and Paul had been back for two weeks, I was still nervous. The other times she had been just as resolute that the relationship was over.

So I worried. What if she did what she had done so many other times?

"Paul," I said, "what if Mom goes back while we're away?"

"She won't. She hates his guts."

"Well I know she says that, but remember. She's said that before. I agree though, Paul, this time it seems different. And she's already been back two weeks. Still, if something happens, see if you can get over to Brian's house. Okay? Just until we get back." Brian had been Paul's best friend since the second grade. A soft-spoken lad, Brian was bigger than any second grader I had ever known. His parents said that when the teacher asked what was the best thing to happen to him that year, he had one word. Paul.

He nodded. "I can pull it off. Don't worry."

> —Paul, do you remember when I gave you that advice about trying to go to Brian's if Mom went back to Mario while we were away?
> —I wasn't going back. If I couldn't get to Brian's and they got the cops to take me, I would just stroll over to the library and ask someone to call DCF.

After spending the Fourth with the gang at Lake George, we drove up to Montreal. Tammy sounded fine whenever I called her, and even spoke enthusiastically about a bracelet she was making. I was enjoying the New England countryside when suddenly Paul called. He said he was in Brian's dad's car. Mario had come over and Tammy said something about a new baby. Brian's dad serendipitously pulled in the driveway to pick up his son as Mario and Tammy were engaged in intense words. Profiting from their inattention to him, Paul jumped in the car with Brian and called me. He laughed triumphantly. The plan had worked. "Are they behind us? No!"

I knew that Tammy couldn't be pregnant- she had an IUD. Still, Mario seemed to believe this because when I got back there was a message on my machine about Paul's new brother. Another phantom child. She must have really wanted Mario back.

I felt helpless. As Don drove north to Canada, I was ill, thinking that they would come to Brian's family with the cops, as usual. Poor Paul – but even if I had been there, I would have been powerless. We had plans in Montreal that filled me with guilt. Karen was coming from Indiana to Canada to meet us. I hadn't spent time with her in so long. We were supposed to enjoy the city while Don went to the conference. How would I enjoy anything?

I talked to Paul and to Brian's mother Amanda every day. I said that if they needed me, I'd get on a plane. They heard nothing from Tammy.

After a few days, Amanda said, "You know, we're not really comfortable giving him back to them. They can bring the cops but we'll resist." So, I relaxed and went with Karen to see the embalmed heart of Brother André and enjoyed the street performances of Cirque du Soleil, meeting up for dinner with Don. The three of us lingered over wine, sharing our lives. Jonathan, Karen's son from Sierra Leone, had a young son named Atticus. We went to Don's panel. Karen said he was the only one who communicated in intelligible English.

We got home, picked Paul up, and waited and wondered if we would hear from Tammy. Paul was going to middle school for sixth grade. A few days before the start of school, I was puttering in the kitchen wondering if I would have any problems with his enrollment papers. Paul was playing over at Brian's. Suddenly Layla alerted and ran to the garage door. There stood Tammy looking drained of emotion, like a body on automatic pilot.

"Hi, Honey."

"Hi, Mom. I just came by to give you this."

"Come on in, Sweetie. How are you?"

She took a few tentative steps inside and proffered a piece of three-ring notebook paper with handwriting on it. I quickly dried my hand to take it and give it a look.

"Here, if you want him, you can have him. That's all I came for."

Her loss of affect was so complete that I thought it must have been a defense against intense suffering. I knew how much she loved Paul.

The paper read: "I give my mother, Margaret Gonzalez, permission to enroll my son, Paul Martin, in school and to take him to the doctor. Tamlyn Martin."

"Tammy, you know I am happy to take care of him. What's going on?"

"Everything is just going so fast. I can't handle it. I can't take care of him AND work on my relationship. "

I had to smile. She always used that line about things going too fast. She must have heard it on a Soap years ago because she'd been saying it since she was a teen.

"Well, that's all I came for," she said.

"Wait a second, Tammy. If you want me to take care of Paul, maybe we should make it more formal." Here was my chance to make sure he was never again snatched away against his will.

"Whatever you want," she said blankly.

"Well, I think he would feel more secure if he knew where he was supposed to be."

"Okay. Sure. If that's what you want. I just can't take care of him right now."

"Tammy, you're his mom. It's just that a legal document would make him feel more secure. Temporary custody."

"I said 'okay.'"

"Okay. I'll call the lawyer and we'll go to his office. Next week. Can I call you or email you?"

For the first time in almost a year I had her email address. Apparently Mario had tired of the child-rearing chore. He brought Tammy to the lawyer's office right on schedule. Her look was still emotionless and world-weary. Mario didn't like the provision that Tammy would have to go to court to regain custody, but he quickly backed off. He saw he was at cross-purposes with himself. When they left, the lawyer said, "I told you that Tammy was the weak link."

Paul flourished. He took the school bus every morning. He started out the year with enthusiasm. He seemed more mature in every way except that at night he felt anxious and wanted to sleep on the couch, with me singing the lullabies he hadn't heard since he was little. We ordered pizza every Friday and Brian, along with half the neighborhood, came over to share it with us.

We read together. I bawled uncontrollably through the ending of *Where the Red Fern Grows.* (The doggies, coonhounds like our own Layla, died. Unbearable). When we followed up with *Old Yeller,* Paul brought out a full box of Kleenex.

"I know you, Grandma."

"Paul," I said, "I miss Mommy. You must too."

"It's just like the song," he said, struggling to control the tremolo in his voice. "She's just Somebody I Used to Know."

In October, just as one of these pizza parties was unfolding, Tammy came by. By the next week, she came home for good.

The day after she arrived, Mario called me. He said, "Let's face it. I was the best thing that ever happened to her. I see it doesn't work for you not to be in the picture. Tell her to come back." It must have cost him something to say this. It would certainly cost me something to put behind me that I was a white trash drunk farm animal.

"I'll tell her what you said, Mario."

I did tell her, but she was done. This time she was really done. "When he calls back, tell him to forget about it."

25

EVOLUTION - OR HOW DID I GET INTO THIS?

In the fall of Paul's sixth grade year, the Director of Religious Education at the church resigned, and since I had already done the job, they asked me to come back as an interim while they conducted a search. The second and third grade class needed a teacher so Don and I decided we'd tackle it ourselves. I wanted to do something based on science and perhaps related to nature. We asked the children if they knew what habitat loss was. They were experts! They also were conversant on such topics as climate change and pollution. But when we asked about evolution, they were stumped. Does it have something to do with revolution?

It turns out that in our county the religious right has such a stranglehold on the science curriculum that the word "evolution" is not permitted. I asked Paul if his science teacher mentioned evolution. "Oh yeah, she says she's such a great science teacher they could never get rid of her for saying the "e" word."

"Good for her, Paul!"

But a less subversive, more compliant teacher could refer only to "changes over time." We now had a mission. I found Connie Barlow's wonderful curriculum, "The Great Story," and set out to convey science's breathtaking chronicle of where we came from.

For our first lesson, I filled a black balloon with glitter, inflated it, and took the kids into the pitch black, windowless men's room. I turned my flashlight on at the precise moment that I burst the balloon, propelling "stardust" into space. We all got to see the Big Bang! (Don't try this at home; you'll be picking up glitter for weeks.)

We had fun making paper mâché dinosaurs and then simulating the extinction event that wiped them out. One kid played the furry critter who sought refuge in a cave, thus allowing life to proceed toward us.

I learned more than the kids. When humans were still hunters and gatherers, wolves were attracted to the discarded carcasses of their kills. The most docile of these wolves hung around and, since they were not aggressive, folks didn't mind. Humans soon found that these beasts were useful because they would sound the alarm if there were any impending invasions. Thus began the long symbiosis of humans and canines. The fittest wasn't always the physically strongest. Survival of the nicest.

But here was my problem. According to Darwinian thought, the dual purposes of life are survival, living now, and reproducing, living on biologically. So where am I? In evolutionary terms, I am at least a 50% failure. On the plus side, I did survive.

This theory provides me with two puzzles: adoption and grandmothering. My genes are lost for the future. The "grandmother hypothesis," an attempt to understand why we go on after we have outlived our evolutionary usefulness, maintains that the postmenopausal woman has the function of helping her reproducing offspring raise their own children, which in our particular species are fragile and need all the help they can get. But this notion leaves out adoption. In all probability, most grandmothers support subsequent generations to keep their own biological inheritance in play.. If raising a biologically alien being is perplexing, helping that being raise her own descendants seems to make no Darwinian sense.

I like to think that natural selection explains everything from the Big Bang and the formation of the solar system to the self-sacrifice of miniscule ants in my kitchen. But adoption adds a layer of complexity. Scientists, through genetic testing, have discovered that some baby birds being raised by ostensibly monogamous pairs are not related to the papa bird. Mama bird's hanky-panky shows that stepparents are just as good as biological ones. Other studies show that some adult fish and birds routinely swap a portion of their fry and their chicks with other adults, thereby cutting down the risk of complete loss of their own. This reciprocal adoption favors survival. Adoption in the wild appears to adhere to Darwin's principles more than human adoption.

Maybe it works like this. As an adaptation for the particularly long period it takes for a human to become an adult, many of us have a longing to nurture. Without this, the baby would be out with the bath water the first time he propelled projectile pee into Mom's eye. Naturally, this feature proves most useful for one's own offspring; after all, they are usually the ones who are there. But suppose some individuals find no mate during their reproductive years, and suppose they have a strong case of that adaptation to nurture. Then suppose there are children available with a need to be fed, housed and generally doted on. Then adoption becomes a means to nurture and a bonus for survival of the species itself.

If I had the power to tinker with evolution, I would expand that part of our DNA that drives us to care for our vulnerable infants, burdened as they are by their big heads housing their outsized brains. I guess I do believe something. I believe that all our empathetic, generous, kind impulses stem from the part of our brain that leads us to nurture the helpless young. Darwin himself contended that sympathy was the strongest of our evolved instincts. I love Ian Brown's poignant idea in his effort to draw meaning from the life of his profoundly disabled child. He speculates that his boy can inspire the rest of us with compassion – that enhanced compassion is perhaps the adaptation that will do most to move the species forward. Survival of the nicest.

But I am not the nicest. What about a step-grandfather and step-father who came on the scene when Paul was nine and Tammy was thirty? Where does he fit in this centripetal force we call family?

Here is the answer from my inspired Sunday School co-teacher, who, in a whirlwind of pedagogic fervor, devoured at least two hundred books on evolution: "I don't know what Darwin would say, but I love Tammy and Paul."

26

HOMESCHOOL

As soon as she came back, Tammy stepped into her mother role. Paul persuaded her to drive him to and from school. He'd had enough of the chaos of the school bus. She was at his beck and call. She also reacquainted herself with Princess and poured her tender affections to the welcoming pooch. Princess went everywhere with her including to the parent pick-up line at the middle school. According to Tammy, everyone wanted the royal dog. "Everybody wants to take you home, don't they, baby. But no. Don't worry. Mommy's not ever going to let you go." And then she'd look at me and say, "Me and Princess have always had a special bond."

She swore off men.

When Paul was finishing up the sixth grade, it became clear that he was in crisis. At a few years distance I see how challenging life must have been for him. Maybe he had a touch of Post-Traumatic Stress. After all, he had gone through two years of being treated like a sack of potatoes, pulled from his stable nest into a wacky unpredictable world. Having already gotten used to his father's absence, he had to adjust to the idea that his mother was somebody that he used to know and then was somebody he had to get used to again. On top of that, his primary supporters were old, and he could see that he would have to look after his mother when we died. This all came along with the normal upheaval of moving from the contained classroom of elementary school to middle school, with its rotating schedule and chaotic hallways.

Into this turmoil came the miracle of the 3D sandbox video game, *Minecraft*. This game captivated him. He lost all interest in anything else. Shooting hoops or taking a dip in the pool were annoying intrusions into the place where true reality resided – the computer screen.

He told me he couldn't take middle school. It was too confusing. He was bullied.

"Please, please, Grandma. You've got to homeschool me."

I have never understood homeschooling. Why would anyone want to insulate their child against the rough and tumble of life? Why would anyone want to sacrifice the work world, with all its stimulations and financial benefits, for life at home with a kid who for absolutely sure would behave more self-indulgently than in school. How many times have I congratulated parents on the exceptional manners of their child only to have them look at each other and say, "Our child?" Kids behave better when they are not with people who will love them anyway. I had taught a group of home schoolers, and they had no idea of how to take turns. I was not a fan of home schooling.

Yet I caved.

"If I do it, you'll have to do something social. "

I gave him a list; he chose the sex ed course called OWL (Our Whole Lives), offered at the church, and Sunday School. He would be with kids on Wednesday evenings and Sunday mornings

Why did I cave? I didn't have a new job lined up, I thought he wasn't learning anything at school, I could teach him more, it would be fun, and it would be great for the whole family. Oh, and my grandson wanted to spend time with me. Are you kidding? There was no real choice.

Tammy did art and sign language with him, and Don did history and science. My job was vocabulary, reading, writing, French, and piano. PE would be either my treadmill or the pool. For the first semester the four of us, sporting Paul Martin Homeschool T-shirts, took a field trip every Wednesday. Museums, nature preserves, and historic walks. We even took an extended field trip to Richmond, Washington and Williamsburg. I will never forgive Ted Cruz and the do-nothing Congress for shutting down the government just as we were going to see the White House and the Air and Science Museum.

It was a fantastic year for learning. Paul memorized Yeats's *Lake Isle of Innisfree*. He wrote a six-page magazine called *Minecraft Nerds*. The whole family watched all the episodes of Cosmos with Neil deGrasse Tyson and then discussed them. We sat with our clipboards taking notes. Tammy amazed me with her ability to pull out the main ideas. She, too, got another bite of the education apple. Paul grasped what a haiku was and how it could capture a Minecraft moment:

Flip a lever
Redstone flames and transforms your house
Magical switch

In April, though, Don suddenly was hit with severe pain in his lower abdomen. He had had colon cancer fourteen years earlier and apparently the radiation came back to make his life intolerable. It took months – too many months – and too many trips to the ER where we begged for a shot of Dilaudid—to get the pain under control. I thought that medical science would help him. But for months he woke every day with pain that shot up to a ten. He tried dives in the hyperbaric chamber, acupuncture, Buddhist meditation, hypnosis, and injections into his back. His only relief was sleep, induced by Ambien. He had always read four or five books a week. Now he was too restless to read at all. He frenetically summarized *New York Times* articles for his puzzled friends on Facebook.

I took Paul to a techy summer camp in Atlanta while Don's daughter Lauri took him to the Mayo clinic for a visit his brother had arranged. Even there, no magic remedy was waiting in their esoteric bag of tricks. It wasn't until late summer, when a pain management doctor in Fort Myers tried a risky injection of pure alcohol into his spine, that a nerve was killed and the pain knocked down to a four. Little by little that four became a zero. My amateur opinion is that those months of suffering triggered the new health problems that surfaced: swollen legs that required a vascular specialist and an irregular heartbeat. So a few more months were spent visiting specialists for treatable new things.

We had planned to homeschool Paul for two years, but I said, "Paul, Grandpa can't help me. Let's just find you a really good school." Tammy concurred that he should go back to school. "He needs the socialism." I homeschooled him that fall while we visited and applied to schools. We were reading *The Curious Incident of the Dog in the Nighttime* when he said, "What are the questions?"

I said, "We have to read the passage first."

"I have read it."

"Well, I haven't."

That's when Paul left his teacher in the dust. He really was reading faster than I was. I figured I'd catch him on comprehension. No such luck. He understood what he read.

27

MISSING FLOYD

Tammy, Paul, and I took a big road trip up to Lake George, New York when Paul was six. When we neared Manhattan I got in touch with Floyd and asked if he would like to have breakfast with us the next morning. It was a Sunday. I remember because we could find parking easily on the street. I found a spot right in front of his building.

He was waiting for us on the stoop, more overweight than before, and wearing a baseball cap to hide his balding head. We headed south a couple of blocks to a restaurant, and it was clear that he was having trouble walking. Paul had so many things he wanted to say to him, but at the sight of Daddy in the flesh, he was struck mute. They looked at each other and smiled. Floyd said he'd had psychiatric problems. He had given up the idea of working. His brain was addled. He was happy to see us.

Now Paul is sixteen. I have heard nothing from Floyd since that last breakfast. He has never contacted Paul. I send him photos from time to time, but I never hear back. Once I found him looking scruffy and worn on Facebook. One of the pictures I had sent him of Paul was there too, a picture of Floyd and Paul on the steps of his building on 24th Street that morning we went to breakfast. They looked unspeakably happy to be together. The next time I looked, he no longer had a page. I sent him a copy of *Minecraft Nerds*. It wasn't sent back, so I guess he got it.

There is one thing I know for sure. Floyd loves Paul and misses him every day. His lack of contact isn't about lack of love. It is about protecting Paul from the sorry circumstances of his life.

Last year, out of the blue, Tammy started to get child support payments. Though the bureaucracies involved are tight-lipped about what happened, between the lines we have gathered that he began to collect disability payments of the kind that are for people who have worked in the past but who are now disabled. At least something came of my pressuring him to stay employed. His disability payment should be over twice as much money as Tammy's SSI.

Last Christmas, we all four went to New York. Our last day, on the way to the airport, Tammy and Paul said they really wanted to find Floyd. I drove them round to the building on 24th Street, and Don and I waited as the car idled in front of a fire hydrant. A man at a desk gave them an apartment number, and they went up and rang the bell. The man who answered was not Floyd. He said he knew nothing about Floyd, and that this was his apartment now.

I tried to message Floyd on Facebook. I check for postings on the internet. I even went into Riker's website. Paul wants to know his dad.

28

TAMMY

"I'm a witch," Tammy told Don one morning. "You didn't know?"

"You're a witch? What does that mean?"

"It's not what you think. A lot of people hear the word *witch* and they assume that this has got to be evil, it must be black magic, it must be casting spells, it must be Satan. NO! It's not about spells. I believe in the earth and the surroundings and that everybody is connected to each other. You respect the earth and love the earth and try to protect the earth. The word has become very distorted. Mom, remember I made a meal from the witch 's cookbook? Well the ingredients come from the earth so when you're making it, you're respecting the earth and you're blessing the ingredients as you go along because this is about blessing things that come from the earth.

"It's like every year at our church we have a blessing of the animals and my coven, that's what we do. We don't cast spells on them. We bless them and thank them for being our companions.

"We bless winter, spring, summer, fall; we bless the different galaxies and the constellations; we bless all the elements, earth, rain, wind, fire so it's a lot more than most people think when they hear the word witch. The word scares some people; they don't want to understand what's behind it."

"Sounds like Unitarian paganism," said Don.

"I love animals and I love the earth, and that's what this religion is about and I believe in it. Yes, it's paganism. That's the religion."

So when you hear the depressing term dull normal, which has been applied to Tammy, it is also not what you think. So many years ago, in Tammy's first report in kindergarten, Jane and Judy praised her exuberance. Poking through the learning challenges, the volatile behavior, and the gloomy face, was a kid with pizzazz. At the Lowell School, she was the queen of Special Ed. One of her friends complained to me that she was tired of Tammy getting all the attention. If things got boring, oh well, she would just liven things up by concocting the story of her purloined child. Pretty soon the whole high school would be ready to march on the courthouse. Livening things up is still her stock in trade.

One day when I brought in the mail, I called to Tammy, "Tammy, you got a package."

"OH YIPPEE YIPPEE YIPPEE." She jumped around, rubbing her hands together.

"What is it?"

"It's the insects I ordered on line. Yum."

"Yuck."

"That's what *you* think. They're the new super food. They're good. They're crunchy. It's like eating a chip. I mean, no ooze comes out of them. They're dehydrated. It's like a crispy cracker only it just has legs and a little antenna."

Indeed, inside the package there were neat packets of dried bugs. She tore open the cellophane and wolfed down a handful. "It's completely safe, you know."

"Just like a cracker only with legs," I said with disgust.

"More like a chip," came the cheery reply. "These look like crickets, but the millipede worms, oh my God, they're really delicious. And the tarantulas – those are the best. You didn't know I liked bugs?"

I don't know why I didn't know. For her whole life, I've watched her suck every last morsel out of any crustacean put before her. Bugs were not too much of a leap. If I gave her chicken salad, though, that exotic fare was just much too gross. "Can't eat it. Sorry, just can't."

She was obsessed by the dolphin Winter, the subject of the film *Dolphin Tale*. Poor Winter lost her tail after she was injured in a crab trap. The movie shows the quest to invent a prosthetic tail for her. Tammy frequently checked the live cam to see how she was doing, and was enthralled by Winter's relationship with another dolphin, Hope.

"What's going on here, Tam?"

"Well, when Winter's adopted mommy Panama died, before they got Hope to replace her, she went under that ladder all the time – it made her feel safe because she lost her mommy. When she was under there she was in distress mode. But now she has Hope. They found Hope when she was just a baby with her mom, who was dead. I mean, poor little Hope was trying to nurse her dead mother. And she was lost from her pod. Okay, I love animals. Sue me."

Tammy got Paul, Don, and me so involved, that we took an excursion up to Clearwater Marine Aquarium. Don and I stood at the edge of the crowd by the dolphin's pool while Tammy and Paul threaded their way up to the front. I could see that Tammy, oblivious to the spectators, was in her own world, communicating with Winter. Then the trainer actually seemed to chat with Tammy.

Don and I watched and then left to look at the other exhibits. When Tammy caught up with us she was flushed with excitement. "Winter was hiding when I got there, you know, under the ladder. And they were trying to get her out from underneath and then I came there and she came out right away and she started doing tricks and stuff. I whistled, and she came right out. And the lady told me I mean the lady said, 'Damn, you're good.' So I told her I'd been watching them and researching them. You have to whistle a certain way, not just a regular whistle and she told me it took her two and a half years to figure that out. And then I do it right off the bat. She told me if I needed a summer job to let her know.

"And once the crowd knew, they were yelling to me, 'Whistle again.' Cuz she was doing flips and everything."

Several months later, I asked Tammy what was the most important thing she learned from studying the dolphins.

"When you have an animal like a porpoise or a whale or a seal or a dolphin, you have to have at least two so they won't be alone. They have to have a companion to play with and hang out with and not be alone and not be isolated."

"Tammy, this is just an idea I have and I might be wrong, but do you think that your interest in Hope and Winter, who were rescued away from their families, has something to do with your own life, when you were rescued away from your family?"

"Probably. Yup. I was pretty young when I was separated but there's still a lot I remember – all the yelling and screaming. There's bits and pieces. I'll see a flash about something and I almost have it figured out and then I get a flash of something else and I go, whoa, what's that flash about?"

"You told me you loved your birth mom."

"How can you not love your mom? Even though she put me through hell there's always part of me that loves her. But being part of my life and loving her a little bit are two separate things. I don't trust her."

"Do you think that if instead of putting you in foster care they gave money to her. . ."

"No. NO. It wouldn't work. My brothers would tell you the same thing. It would not work because she would take that money straight to drugs. That was her support for dealing with my father. He would come home and say, 'You bitch buh buh buh buh buh' and she would go straight to the drugs and the liquor and drink and smoke herself until she passed out. That's why Steven and Chris basically raised me and my siblings – because Mom would be passed out."

"So what do you think about foster care?"

"Been there done that. It sucks."

"In what way?"

"Not everyone gets adopted. And sometimes they get so screwed up because of the whole system of trying to get adopted and then not getting adopted and they're either in jail or homeless or they're on the streets because of the fact that the system failed them. They're waiting and waiting and after they get of adult age and they've never been adopted the system doesn't help them to find a house to live in or a job to support them. As soon as they turn of age they tell them to leave, and when you have no support it isn't easy. You turn to drugs or selling drugs and that sends you to jail or if you're a female you start hooking yourself to make money so that you can have a place to live in. And that can lead to diseases or unwanted pregnancies. It's a ticking bomb waiting to happen."

"Tammy, do you have dreams for the future?"

"I hope my kid gets a nice girlfriend and I just hope he finds a nice strong relationship with nice friends when he goes to college because that boy's going to college whether he likes it or not and I hope he finds a job he enjoys."

"Honey, those are hopes and dreams for Paul. What about you?"

"I'll be happy if I can survive to be forty."

"What are you talking about? You're almost thirty-eight. It seems a pretty sure thing you'll make it to forty."

"My body is slowly deteriorating. I'm always sick and never get well."

"Tammy, Honey, you have a cold. You'll be well next week."

"Well, forty is the next milestone. After than maybe I'll think about fifty."

29

GIVE ME OXYGEN

My sleep was interrupted by my husband's frequent trips to the bathroom. He was preparing for a colonoscopy, so he had no choice. A little before 6 AM, I took him to the doctor and then went home. I knew I should wait with him. He had to be anxious. He was experiencing new intermittent pain. After some spinal shots the year before, he thought he was done with the pain. But I had to get back home to walk the dog and wake up my fifteen-year-old grandson.

At 7:00 the hound and I took our daily trek around the block. It was necessary to go at 7:00 at the very latest because otherwise we might meet the two giant poodles, which activated Layla's feral ancestry. If we met them, the entire neighborhood would be awakened by desperate, loud, staccato barks, which I understood to mean, "There are poodles, I tell you. Alert the National Guard, sound the alarm. Poodles, I say. Do you hear me?" After the frantic barking, Layla would throw back her head to bay mournfully. If we had a heath, her wails would resound over the desolate moor. Any opossums or raccoons that heard her, would doubtlessly cower across the road in the abandoned golf course. I would be panting as fifty-five pounds of muscle tried to drag me toward the stylish pair, who continued on their way, noses held high, indifferent to the crazed beast.

This morning we left at 7:00, right on schedule, at least a half hour before the elegant duo usually put in their appearance. During the walk, I tried to gather my strength for the next event – waking Paul. For six weeks waking Paul had not been going well. Every morning, if he emerged from his coma-like state at all, he said he didn't feel well. Nothing I did would persuade him to get up for school. I took him to the doctor twice. They did cultures and blood work and told him to go to school.

He had gone back to his old middle school for the second semester of 8th grade. His attendance was so terrible that Tammy, Paul, and I were all formally requested to attend a meeting with the police in downtown Fort Myers. An officer explained to Paul that now that he had turned fourteen, he was responsible for his attendance. If he were to miss any more school, he would likely go to jail.

"I'm sorry, Paul, but we do not have two facilities – one for non-violent offenders like you and one for the sort of kids who attack innocent homeless people and commit other acts of violence. I guess you heard about the homeless man who got beat up last week. Well, the teen who committed that assault is right here, on the other side of this wall. " I looked at Paul. He was wiping away tears that were streaming down his face. The officer had gotten his attention. Paul was great for the rest of 8th grade. Scared straight.

Then he went into a new tailspin when he entered the large nearby public high school for 9th grade. History was repeating itself. Shades of his mother at Murry Bergtraum.

He wrote me a sixteen-page paper entitled WHY I HATE HIGH SCHOOL. He complained of bullying and mean teachers. *"I just wanna be in a nice peaceful and noise free environment to sit down and do all my work and succeed in life and become a better person."*

"As I'm writing this I am actually crying about what I am saying, all of it is true and just makes me think more and more about how bad my life actually is. Every day I just dream that my Grandma will see how bad life really is right now for me and see that I'm not making excuses . . .I would love to be in Online Courses. I would love to learn some art stuff from my Mom and some French from my Grandma and then learn more about Psychology from my Grandpa if he's up to it . . .Mom read this and said, "That was deep and that must have come from the heart."

I fell for it. I yanked him out of high school and found a miraculous little private school that we could afford. I sweetened the deal by volunteering to teach a French class. Then he refused to go.

I had been so sure that my behavior modification plan would work. After all, he loved money. On a calendar, I wrote $15 on each Monday. My scheme was to reward attendance and penalize absence. If he missed school, three dollars was subtracted. If he went, three dollars was added. I remembered bitterly, as Layla and I passed the lot where the burrowing owls lived, that the first day of this plan he refused to get up. He seemed to think that money was no good if you had to do anything to get it. "What's wrong with this boy?" I asked Layla. She took a break from sniffing the grass to train her big brown sympathetic eyes on me.

So after taking Don for his procedure and walking Layla, I approached Paul's room feeling a familiar dread. All I expected of him was that he go to school. Not too much to ask. Not at all. I turned off the lava lamp and turned on the light. I looked at the sleeping boy and took a moment to love him before anger gripped me and made me ill with effort.

"Paul, it's time to get up." He did not stir.

"Paul, come on Honey. You have to wake up. It's time for school." No answer.

"Paul! Honey! Remember you said you would go to school today?" No answer.

"Paul. PAUL! Okay, I'm going to shake you. Come on!"

I shook him and started to count the shakes. When I got to 50, I took a self-pity break. I felt powerless. Since he was born, I was determined to provide the environment that would launch him into a productive life. But so much of him was opaque to me. I worried that like his father he would take what myopia sees as an easy path but in the full bloom of time leads only to abject poverty. The vision of a homeless Paul gave me a second wind.

"Paul, would you wake up? Wake up. Wake up." I slapped his blanket where I thought his legs might be. "Come on. Come on you little bastard. Get the fuck up. How much do you think Ms. Kris is going to put up with? You're going to get yourself kicked out of that school and then what will you do? I'll have to put you back in Ida Baker High and you'll end up in jail with the teenage axe murderers."

He paid me as much mind as the poodles did Layla.

"Paul. Get up. I can't take this, you creep. I'm getting water to pour on your head.

"Tammy," I called down the hall. "I'm going to get water. Help me if he knocks me out." Tammy and I were often a tag team.

"Oh God, I hate you," I said, my voice near hysteria. "You couldn't care less. Do you know what self-indulgence means?"

I grabbed the blanket he was clutching in his possum mime. Ha, I thought. I got it. I noticed slight movement. "I'm going to make your lunch, Paul. Be ready when I come back." Just to be sure, I left my IPad with a YouTube rendition of a smoke detector on full blast.

As I walked to the kitchen, the nurse called to let me know I should pick up Don. "Wow, already?" I said.

I called to Tammy, "I have to pick up Don. If you can get Paul up, take him to school." As I grabbed the keys, I heard her screaming, shaking him, and cursing the day she had ever given birth to him. I could see she would have no more success than I had.

The doctor didn't find anything alarming in Don's insides. "There is a God," I said. But then I realized there was no explanation for his recurrent pain. "Oh dear," I said. "I made a mistake. There is no God."

"You're pretty fickle on the subject."

"Seemingly. But now I'm thinking that maybe God is a comet that comes around every 600 years or so. That would explain Buddha, then 600 years later, Jesus of course, and then 700 years later—was it 700?—Mohamed."

"Comets come at very regular intervals," he said. "I think the theory needs more work."

"You're right, because I can't think of any big religious discovery in 1400. Would Martin Luther count?"

"There's bound to have been something," he said.

When we got home it was 8:30. Paul was sleeping soundly. At 10:00 I went through the whole dreadful scene again. I teach his French class at the school at 10:40. "Paul, get up. You have to come to French class. What the heck am I teaching this class for if you don't come to it?"

He had won the first battle, but I won the second. He dragged himself to school for French.

In class, he was cooperative and engaged. Naturally. Just as he would be all day long if he actually went to school. I played a song—Celine Dion singing *Oxygène*. The refrain was *Donnez-moi de l'oxygène*. Give me oxygen. Paul said he sympathized because of his asthma. I said I sympathized because I nearly died from a grape lodged in my throat. Someone had saved me by performing the Heimlich maneuver. Another student said she sympathized because she, like Celine, had experienced a panic attack.

Paul refused to stay at school after French, claiming illness. Ms. Kris said he should stay, but he said "No," and got in the car. We stopped at the vet's on the way home, and he helped me find special light diet food for Princess so that her excess weight wouldn't cause her to go into respiratory failure. He promised to go to school the next day. Often when he says that, it's true. Cautiously, I allowed myself to hope.

When this boy is sweet it's as though your Aleve kicks in and your headache disappears. He was spontaneously helpful. He typed up and posted the recommended food quantities for each dog. How pitiful I was. My happiness hung on the whim of a rebellious youth.

The next morning, the morning of the day he promised to go to school, I found a note. "You're going to hate me like always but my asthma at around 10 PM was acting up really severe." After a few more somatic complaints, he said, "I am not tough and strong like you. I never tough things out. I just haven't learned how to yet. I am a weakling." His last point was, "I can always make up work, but I can't make up my health if it gets severe enough."

I subtracted three dollars on his calendar. The boy was too much for me. Strong like me! What a laugh! I felt the irony. My twenties and thirties were consumed with this longing to raise children and the fervent belief that I would be good at it, that I would produce original, brilliant, beautiful beings. My identity would be defined by my superior child-rearing. I would excel at this most womanly art, the art of taking the raw matter of immature life and kneading it, molding it, shaping it until it becomes a joyful, productive, fully realized entity.

I should have learned with Tammy. I should have been humbled into a sure sense of the limits of parenting. But no. My groundless optimism had no bounds. I welcomed a second chance. I still harbored the thought that if I had been there for Tammy – and also for Floyd – from their infancy, things would have been better. Maybe not. Maybe they would have been worse. Stuck in my head was Celine Dion's plaintive cry: *Donnez, donnez-moi, donnez-moi de l'oxygène.*

30
CONSIDER THE GODDAMN LILIES

It seems that the lesson I keep hearing over and over is to give up. You want Tammy to function like a normal person in the real world? Forget about it. You want your grandson to go to school. Uh-uh. And yet, if I could have my way, if aging, death and disease could be banished forever, I would be happy to go on just as we are. Just as we are, four people bound together in a family.

Tammy has become a devoted mother. She can look forward to a life of poverty because she has not learned to earn a living. Back when Paul was in preschool, she finished a program to become a nail tech. She got the state license. I think I took her to every manicure salon in Lee County. She never got past the interview.

I said, "Maybe it's because of your disability."

"But I don't tell them about my disability."

I didn't know what to say to that, so I said nothing.

We went to a job rehab place and got her a job coach. She went around to supermarkets filling out forms. Nothing ever came of her efforts. So for all of our sakes I have let go on the work front.

She is sweet in a grumbling, sardonic way. She is pretty. She loves her son, and she loves Don. She calls him Dad. She confides in him – often about the burdens I put on her. She has a regular job with us doing the laundry every Thursday. As competent as she is with collecting, washing and folding, she keeps up a frustrated patter all day long. "Still another load in the dryer." "I'm exhausted." 'WHO IS WEARING ALL THESE SOCKS?" She helps keep the household functioning, unloading the dishwasher every day and cooking steak every other week. She has casual friendships with the people who work at CVS and 7-Eleven.

Recently I mentioned that when I was thirty, I went to Japan on vacation. After a long flight back, stopping in Alaska and Canada, we arrived at JFK. My brother picked me up, and on our way home from the airport, we heard on the radio that a plane had crashed at JFK. It turns out that it was the plane I had just gotten off of. When I told this story, I heard Tammy gasp. "What is it? "

"I can't imagine life with another mother."

Every night we email each other messages full of emojis before we go to sleep. The night of the French election I said "The better candidate won in France ▮▮ ♥ night night ☽ ."

She immediately answered, "That's awesome!✶✵ for▮▮. I wish them all the best. ♨ ☯is ✿already. Good luck ❋ in ▮▮ class tomorrow. Good ☾ and ◑◑ in the ☀ !"

I can't imagine life with another daughter.

Every day she dances in the garage. Perhaps she has an audience, but they are not people who call or who seek her out. She makes jewelry in her room. She orders magazines and knows everything about the royal family and the movie stars. She is a walking catalog of movies, their actors and the actors' loves.

Princess is her baby. She dotes on her and in return, the royal dog gives her solace. Her son loves her, but since she does not understand how to require him to do anything, she is his virtual slave. When her SSI money comes in, he uses it before she can because he has a PayPal number linked to her bankcard. If he is sitting at his computer and decides he want a glass of water, he says, "Mom, I want a glass of water," and she goes to the kitchen and brings him back one.

I worry about Tammy's future inordinately. I can only leave her what I have, and I don't have enough to support another person for a lifetime. She will inherit a place to live, but she will not have the money to keep it up. I am counting on Paul to help her. For a while I wondered if he had it in him.

I thought that Paul was staying home from school because he wanted to play on his computer. He finally was referred to a psychiatrist who said that he had social anxiety. She prescribed a pill. Paul said his own goal in treatment was to go back to school, but I wasn't taking any chances. I told him that if he missed school I would call a realtor and sell the house. He and his mom could live in some crummy rental and Grandpa and I would go to a place where they serve meals. I would say goodbye to cooking every night for a family of four. I wasn't kidding.

Seven months have passed. A new school year is well under way. Ms. Kris proposed that I teach a larger French class, only not as a volunteer, but in exchange for Paul's tuition. My plan is to stay on this side of the grass long enough for Paul to grow up. I eat lots of veggies and walk Layla for a half hour every day, so I think I'll make it. He knows I plan to pass the torch to him to look out for his mother. He loves her and he's savoring the power.

I am dense at learning the lesson of giving up. I'm pretty sure that's a good thing, Maybe I had to wait until the summer of my seventieth year to find true love, but if I'd given up, I wouldn't have found it at all, now would I? I wouldn't have been paying attention when this exceptionally caring and sensitive – oh, and did I forget to say handsome - man walked into church behind me, telling a friend he had a blind date. I wouldn't have said to myself, let's not be stupid, and then gone home and sent him an email entitled "Stir Crazy," which he has kept to this day.

And perhaps Paul would not have put his anxiety behind him and come to this new place where he loves school and has made new friends. He's had perfect attendance for four months. He's one of my best French students. I go by his room and hear him humming "Alouette." He's taken to calling me "Grand-mère." Every weekend our house is the boys club with old friends like Brian and new ones from the school crashing on our couch.

I don't want to think of what would have happened to Tammy if I had given up on her. She is close enough to normal, whatever that is, to be able to do all things except make a living. Don feels that she has made peace with the way things are and when I die, and she needs money, she'll be able to find a path forward. *Take no thought of the morrow.* As a Clooney character said, "Consider the lilies of the goddamn field."

We have been married for eight years. Logan, the young son of my nephew, Andy, met Don when we were on our honeymoon. "What's next?" he asked me.

"Happily ever after, I guess," I said.

"Oh," he said. "Like Shrek."

"Yes, exactly like Shrek."

Thank you, Dreamworks. You opened the doors of enchantment to all forms and sizes. And all ages, too.

We are old, the time in life when the past lengthens and sprouts in complexity while the future contracts like shrink-wrap. Though *ever after* is so different from *forever*, I feel bathed in the happy present.

So here is what happily ever after looks like. Don is in his trusty recliner reading a chapter on *Brief Strategic Family Therapy*, I am propped on the bed (with Princess burrowing under the blanket and Layla sleeping at my feet) reading yet another memoir, this time about grandparents who get back to childrearing because of the death of their daughter, Paul is in his room playing Steam, and Tammy, who did for me what I dreamed a child would do –gave meaning to the arc of my life—is in the garage, ear buds in her ears, dancing.

EPILOGUE

When Tammy was in high school, I took her uptown to Payne Whitney Psychiatric Clinic for a second opinion. They spent several hours with her and then came out and told me, "It's something, but we don't think it's PDD."

"Well, what is it?"

"We don't know."

Recently, when I asked Tammy what she thought her disability was she said, "I can't take stress."

I think she's right. One therapist said it was more like PTSD than PDD. She still has residual effects of her early trauma. All the love and energy I have directed toward her mitigates but does not remedy. When she's overwhelmed she stops eating for days or runs out into the real and dangerous world in the dark of night worrying me and anyone who might be here. She has severe bouts of anxiety and depression. She spends too many hours alone in her room.

She, like Floyd, is a graduate of the foster care system, perhaps the most psychologically damaging institution that exists apart from war. Not that it is designed to be damaging. In fact, things have improved in the last two centuries. Before the philanthropist, C. Loring Brace, stepped in to found Children's Aid Society in the 19th century, tens of thousands of kids struggled to survive unsupported on the streets of New York and other cities. He sent them off to farm families in the mid-west on Orphan Trains. He claimed, "There are many spare places at the table of life." So the system began whereby children at least slept inside and had sustenance.

But children have more needs than food and shelter. While the system cannot be blamed for failing to undo the damage inherent in the circumstance of abuse or abandonment, it is deeply at fault in not treating entry into foster care as the emergency it is. Being abandoned once is bad enough. Being treated so badly that the state had to step in to save your life is bad enough. But allowing this to occur repeatedly? As a society, we are terribly at fault. Tammy was abandoned at least five times before she came to me. Five times she thought she was on terra firma only to discover it was a sinking raft.

I got into this because I wanted a child. I happened to land in a place where I learned something important: if we address the problem of foster care we will cure much of what ails our society.

Foster care is everyone's problem, right up there with racism and sexism. The big difference is that women and members of minority groups can advocate for themselves. Will we have a three-year-old Martin Luther King or Susan B. Anthony? Will some brilliant eight-year-old orator stand on the steps of the Lincoln Memorial and declare to a sea of children and adults, "I have a dream that all little boys and all little girls, all children everywhere, will have at least one grown-up wholly devoted to making them feel they belong at the table of life"?

Probably not. More than with any other oppressed group, it is up to all of us to lead the charge. We all benefit if we intervene in a timely way. Fewer criminals, fewer homeless people, fewer youth forced into prostitution. It just makes sense. When do we want to pay, pre-suffering or post-suffering?

I imagine a father attacking his addicted wife. I see the police come to arrest him as two little children cower behind the dilapidated sofa. I see the cops say, "We have to do something with these kids," and then whisk them off to the exhausted social worker about to go home at the end of a long day. I see her look at the kids with annoyance. "Oh, God, are there a couple of beds left at the emergency shelter?"

I see the terrorized kids, ripped from everything they have ever known now feeling guilty because they seem to have done something wrong. Here is the birth of traumatic stress.

Well, I have a dream. We fund a Catchers in the Rye Corps of young adults who staff summer camp-like facilities. They are there all the time so kids can be told, "Guess what! You're going to a fun camp for a few days!" And then stoke up the campfire, get out the guitars and sing, "Jimmy's a flower, a beautiful flower. Jimmy's a flower in the garden of life." And then pop a s'more in his mouth. Dial down the trauma and dial up the warmth.

Then give the system plenty of money so that well-trained case workers, with modest caseloads, can expedite placement and assess early on if the biological parents can meet parenting goals. I think of those thick books, a page for each of the thousands of children aching for a permanent home, each of them longing for the love and acceptance of a family. Why are they left to suffer in temporary placements or in group settings where their caretakers come and go? Why do we tolerate this squandering of human potential?

When you kick open the giant, overripe spaghetti squash of Injustice in America, at the center, in the squishy seaweed like goop, you find a tangled mess of society's ills: Poverty, Prejudice, Crime, Discrimination, Ignorance. Lurking in the goo are such horrors as sex trafficking, homelessness, despair, and suicide. If those slimy fibers were color-coded, we could all see that the stain of abuse, neglect and abandonment of children marks every strand.

The community can lend a hand. Generous old folks who volunteer to be guardians *ad litem* for foster kids do make a difference, but the support they provide is small in comparison with what a parent would do. Church drives to give foster kids bikes and dolls for Christmas offer important moments of joy, but a moment is not enough.

What would be enough? Of course we should improve the system itself. But great social workers and lots of money can only do so much. When it becomes clear that the biological family cannot be reconstituted, then there must be caring adults for all of these kids. We need adults who will make a permanent commitment to every single one of them. They need to be adopted forthwith.

That's it. That's the solution. And there is no shortage of people wanting kids. Women and men are willing to spend thousands on in vitro treatments and surrogate mothers. Doesn't it seem strange that people are so keen on reproducing themselves when real young humans are yearning for parents? And pro-life people should put down their placards and take home a foster child. That's when I'll take seriously their commitment to children and life.

"Oh," one might say, "those kids are trouble. Look at how much trouble you've had with Tammy."

Trouble, sure. But also joy. And have you noticed that biological kids are often trouble? Tammy was trouble all right. There will more trouble to come I'm sure. But as the great Greek philosopher Zorba said, "Only death is no trouble."

I have experienced and do appreciate the mindset that yearns for babies who will blossom into great scientists or artists or tycoons, someone just like me only better. But that isn't really parenting. *Parenting is doing the best you can with the real live breathing child in front of you.* Needlepoint that! Saving one child is more than most achieve in a lifetime. Isn't it worth considering?

I'm thinking of all the single women and men who would make great moms and dads. Or the loving couple with fertility issues. Maybe dreams can be amended. Before spending thousands on treatments, a person or couple might consider at least looking at those books, those binders of children, who tragically are reduced to advertising themselves to get a mom or dad, to stating that they love to read and to help in the kitchen so that you will pick them. Is there really something more compelling than saving a young human from homelessness, prison, or prostitution? Here's a platform to run on: *Be a Catcher. Save one child from falling off the cliff.*

Do you think I regret raising Tammy? Here is the truth. I have never regretted casting my lot with this precious person, not for one second. Even during those few dark episodes when I thought our lives would have to end, that our hell was unendurable because her little soul was drowning in depression untouched by any pill or any treatment, even through the misery of the Mario days, even then, I loved her.

This is my baby. I'm glad I got her when she was five. I wish it had been earlier. I wish she had less traumatic stress haunting her life. My valiant Tammy dances or skates her way out of deep funks.

For more information on fostering or adopting children from the foster care system check out these websites.

Adoption from foster care - AdoptUSKids

How to Adopt a Waiting Child from the U.S. Foster Care System

For more information about

Margaret Gonzalez
and
Body In Space
please visit:

www.margegonzalez.net

48975540R00146

Made in the USA
Columbia, SC
14 January 2019